MARK BARBE

URBAN LEGENDS

AN INVESTIGATION INTO THE TRUTH
BEHIND THE MYTHS

summersdale

URBAN LEGENDS UNCOVERED

Summersdale Publishers Ltd
46 West Street
Chichester
West Sussex
PO19 1RP
UK

www.summersdale.com

Printed and bound in Great Britain

ISBN: 1-84024-554-9
ISBN 13: 978-1-84024-554-7

Disclaimer

Acknowledgements

This project has taken four years to complete, and would not have been possible without the help, support and patience of the following people:

Joanna, my parents, Jayne, Whizz, Nan, Jennifer Barclay (for making this possible), Prof. Jan Harold Brunvand, Pep, Patrick Arink (broodjeaap.nl), Sofia Knapp (Valmyndigheten), Maud Gehrman, NG Dave, David Adams and the rest of my friends and family – you know who you are!

This book is dedicated to…

Holly and Harry

CONTENTS

www.project2067.com

INTRODUCTION

When I was about 14, my friend David Adams related an incident that had happened to his father. He had bought a KFC bucket before entering the cinema to watch a film. As the lights dimmed, he took out a piece of chicken and bit into it. Immediately, something oozed down his chin. He ran into the Gents and looked in the mirror, seeing blood running from his mouth. When he inspected the 'chicken' he was eating, he realised it was a battered rat! I couldn't believe it when I read Alex Garland's *The Beach*, where the main character describes the existence of the beach as a 'Kentucky Fried Rat story', meaning it was an urban legend, and then proceeds to tell a story similar to the one told to me by my friend David. I was amazed, as I always believed this had really happened to my friend's father. When I searched the Internet, I found out that it was a story that was told all over the world. From that moment on I was fascinated by urban legends.

Urban legends (ULs) are tales of modern folklore that can be passed on through traditional methods such as word of mouth or by modern methods such as e-mail, faxes, and the Internet. It is not known how the term 'urban legend' was coined, but folklorists have been collecting and studying them for over fifty years. Variations of the same UL can be heard in many different countries, spontaneously spreading like a virus and often adapting themselves to the environment they are told in, with details being localised by the storyteller. ULs often play on the fears, beliefs and anxieties of a particular period or moment in time, and over the years the legends adjust to reflect the themes of the new era and make them more believable. For example, The Vanishing Hitch-hiker (file HR4704 on the website that accompanies this book) is a classic and one of the oldest ULs. In the story, the mode of transport has changed over the years to adapt with the times; from horseback and horse and chariot in the early legends, to the horse and wagon, and eventually to a car in modern versions. If the modern story stuck to the horse and wagon as the mode of transport it simply would not be relevant enough to sustain interest in this day and age.

Because ULs are frequently a sign of the times, they often contain morals or lessons that are embedded within the tale. It may be possible to use the influence of ULs as a manipulation and propaganda tool for political motives, a clever marketing ploy or for more sinister gains. This is an area that I hope to tap into and in which to uncover some truths.

What intrigues me most is how and where the legends originate from, and how they are spread. These are the questions that will be at the heart of my investigation.

The answers to these questions are not as straightforward as you may think, since the teller normally believes the legend to be totally true. The teller will probably say that he/she has heard the story from someone they know (i.e. a friend or relative), and if you asked the friend/relative about the story, they would probably tell you it has actually happened to someone they know. The same pattern will repeat itself again and again, leading to a dead end at every turn and the investigator around the bend. When my friend David recently asked his father about the Kentucky Fried Rat story, his father told him that it had actually happened to an old work colleague of his that he is no longer in contact with. I am sure that if I managed to contact this man, he would tell me that it had actually happened to a friend or relative of his, and so it would go on. It is this complicated network of connections that led the author Rodney Dale to coin the term 'a friend of a friend' (FOAF) in his book *The Tumour in the Whale*.

Tracing the origins of the legends can therefore be a frustrating business, even more so because the legends have a habit of mutating over the years, and so may have originally recounted a totally different set of events to which they do now. Not all ULs are an impressive work of fiction; some are true and others contain an element of truth. Sometimes the border between fiction and reality is blurred so much it is impossible to tell one from the other. As they (don't ask me who) say, the truth can be stranger than fiction.

This brings me nicely to the hotly-debated question 'How can a UL be true if it is just a legend?' There are convincing opinions on both sides of this argument but I believe that ULs are a unique class of legend which must not be confused with 'ordinary' (and overtly fictional) legends. Whether the tale is true or not has no relevance to its classification as a UL. The main difference between ordinary legends and ULs is the method and speed at which a UL circulates to a wide audience, being told and retold, often with small variations (such as being localised) as it is passed from one person to another like in the game Chinese Whispers.

In my investigation I have only identified a UL to be true if I believe that the origin can clearly be defined and there is enough evidence based on my research to support this. If the legend's origins cannot be clearly defined and there is not enough evidence to say if the UL is either true or false, I have given a verdict of 'Undecided'. Where possible I have clearly stated the origins of the legend. A false verdict is only given when there is enough evidence to suggest that the UL cannot possibly be true.

ULs can cover every subject imaginable and, like jokes, seem to arrive on the scene immediately after an important event has happened. Moreover, ULs are thriving with the use of modern technology. The spread of the legends, which used to be reliant on the word of mouth method, has now accelerated thanks to faxes, e-mail and the Internet. This gives the legends an instant global audience. The flip side is that the new technology is very vulnerable to hoaxes. ULs in particular have fed on the fear of computer viruses, spreading worldwide panic over something that is nothing more than a joke.

If you thought this was going to be a nice bedtime story you could read while sipping your hot cocoa in bed, you are in for a shock. Wake up and smell the coffee. You are now part of this investigation. So, sharpen your mind and be prepared to think.

This is how it will work. The ULs are split up into different categories, which I have chosen from across a wide spectrum to give an insight into the fascinating and varied world of ULs. These are the ULs that have made me sit up and take notice and which I think best represent their particular category. Each UL investigation will contain at least one version of the story. The ULs have been gathered from a wide range of sources over the last four years including books, the Internet, newspaper cuttings, and straight out of my inbox from e-mails that I have received.

The journey starts with the Classic Horror category. You will recognise many of these ULs and they will probably feature in your DVD collection (unless your collection consists solely of Disney films), as they are the staple diet of any respectable slasher/horror Hollywood movie (and some not so respectable). Such films include the *Scream* series, the *Urban Legend* films and *Candyman*, to name just a few.

Other categories under the spotlight include Crime, Animals and Pests, Comic Relief, Food and Drink, and Around the World. I also look at the UL phenomenon of Netlore. This category has special relevance to this investigation as it demonstrates the fusion of ULs and the Internet, providing an unsettling look at how reputations can be destroyed or tainted, and how businesses and governments can be manipulated and brought to their knees with one click of a mouse button. Not only is this the age of information, it is also the age of misinformation.

Another vital but controversial category is 9/11. In these times of uncertainty and paranoia, ULs are used as a balancing force to try and make sense of an inconceivable situation. More disturbingly, they can be used as propaganda either to justify acts in the war against terror or as a smokescreen designed to cause confusion and blur the lines between fact and fiction.

www.project2067.com is the official website for this book and has been created to give you a more interactive experience, containing selected ULs from this book as well as a Special Features section where you will find additional ULs. Each UL in this book has been assigned a unique code, which can be used as a shortcut to access that particular UL on the website. There you will find further information on these ULs, such as different versions of the story, different endings, and different theories about the tale's origin. Not only will you be able to send in your own findings, arguments and opinions, you will also be able to view what other readers have sent in.

Do you know a different version, and where and when did you first hear it? More importantly, do you know any arguments on the origins and theories behind the ULs? Do you know if they are true or false, and if they are false, why were they started and how? With your help, I will uncover the shroud of mystery that surrounds the purpose and origins of these legends.

Now, I know what you are thinking. Why should you bother to help me? Well, if you had no knowledge of ULs beforehand, I am sure you will become as intrigued by the subject as I was when I first came across them, so jump on board for the journey and I will take you to some interesting and far out places en route. Let's go 'smoke' some urban legends.

CATEGORY: CLASSIC HORROR

I consider this category the bread and butter of ULs. These tales offer horror in its simplest and purest form, delivered straight to the heart like an adrenalin rush. They form the backbone to most modern horror stories, and today's slasher/horror films are heavily dependent on and influenced by these gruesome tales. They survive the hands of time for one simple reason; they make good storytelling. A cub scout campfire would be meaningless without at least one of these ULs being told while heating marshmallows over the open flames. Then after the campfire, in the tent with your friends, huddled into your sleeping bag once the darkness of night has settled in, you lay awake, replaying the stories like an old B-movie in your mind. Dark shadows slipping over the tent, the hoot of an owl followed by scuffling noises from the nearby wood… Are those footsteps you can hear? Is that a hook you can make out from the shadows crawling across the canopy?

After reading the Bloody Mary story I dare you (no, no – I double-dare you) to say the name five times while looking in a mirror. You know the story isn't true, but bogeymen do exist, and are lurking somewhere in the back of your mind. ULs tap into this basic fear and exploit it, and that is what makes them so effective.

So without further delay, let's move on. Best not be late, for you have a date with the bogeyman…

Name:	Back-seat Hitch-hiker
Code:	HR4701
Origin:	1967, USA
Status:	False

UNCOVERED

The Legend: Version 1

As a girl is driving back home along a dark country lane after a night out with the girls in Bracknell, Berkshire (England), she comes across a dog lying in the middle of the road. Being an animal lover, she immediately stops and dashes over to the dog to see if it is dead or just injured. Whilst approaching the dog, the headlights of a car appear in the distance behind her. After a quick examination of the creature she realises it is dead and moves the body to the side of the road.

By now the other car is near, so she rushes back to her car and pulls away swiftly. As soon as she does this, the car behind accelerates so that it is right up behind her. The girl looks in her rear-view mirror to see the male driver making hand gestures of some kind at her. He then starts beeping his horn and continuously flashing his lights. By now the girl is petrified and accelerates even more to try and shake off the nutter. The pursuer keeps up, still flashing his lights and beeping his horn.

This pursuit carries on for another couple of miles before the girl finally reaches home, and speedily pulls up onto her drive. She immediately rushes into her house; double-locks the door and rushes to the window. The man who had pursued her was now running up her drive. He reaches her car just as another man is climbing out from her back seat. The pursuer grapples the man to the floor and motions to the girl to call the police. The police arrive promptly and arrest the man who had climbed out from the back seat of her car.

Later, the man in the pursuing car tells the police that he had spotted a man climb into the back seat of the girl's car when she had been attending to the dead dog. He had followed her frantically trying to catch her attention. Every time he saw the man's head bob up from the back seat, he had beeped his horn and flashed his lights to put him off. The man in the back seat has now been taken back to the jail he escaped from, where he is serving a sentence for murder.

The Legend: Version 2

It was a dark and foggy night. A girl was driving home alone and was so tired she could hardly keep her eyes open. She was finding it difficult to concentrate on the wet road, her petrol indicator was on red, and she didn't know where the next petrol station was. She had just about given up hope of finding a petrol station when she spotted one in the near distance and pulled in. It seemed almost derelict, but a petrol attendant came out of his office and slowly approached the car. The attendant's eyes were darting all over the place and he seemed very distracted when she asked him to fill her car up. As he did so he kept looking over at the girl in a way that gave her the creeps. After he had finished, the girl handed over all the money she had, which happened to be the exact cost the petrol came to. The attendant told her it was not enough and that she would have to step into his office. The girl felt increasingly worried as she followed him into the small office, knowing that the amount she had given him was correct. As soon as she stepped into the office the attendant slammed the door shut behind her, and she felt like she was going to scream. The attendant hurriedly explained that he had to drag her away from the vehicle as he had observed a man crouching down in her back seat, and didn't want the man to realise that he had been spotted.

The attendant called the police who arrived promptly and arrested the man. The girl later found out that the man was a wanted serial killer, and had stowed away in her car waiting for the right moment to pounce.

The Investigation

Although this UL originates from the USA, I first heard Version 1, which is set in my neighbouring county (Berkshire), when I was very young, and this UL has been doing the rounds in one format or another for many years. It is believed that the legend first entered the scene in 1967, becoming one of the most popular horror stories of that period. Although versions do vary, the core elements of this UL remain the same; the intended victim is always female and always misreads the intentions of the male rescuer. The rescuer is always astute, either luring the female away from danger, or beeping his horn and flashing his lights every time the madman pops up from the back seat, forcing him back into hiding. The stranger in the back seat is always male, and either a lone madman/serial killer, or part of a gang initiation. His intentions are rarely clearly defined, and you are left to draw your own conclusions.

And Finally...

Although it is a popular belief amongst folklorists that there are grains of truth in this UL, I believe that it was originally told as a warning to lone females to be vigilant when travelling at night. It is also a story of stereotyping, with the lone female always jumping to the wrong conclusion about the rescuer's intentions, not realising the real danger was much closer than she thought.

Name:	The Hook
Code:	HR4702
Origin:	Mid 1950s, USA
Status:	Undecided

UNCOVERED

The Legend

A young teenage couple are driving to a remote Lovers' Lane when a news flash interrupts the song on the radio announcing that a serial killer has just escaped from the local prison, and is considered extremely dangerous. The announcer warns people to stay in their houses and not to go out unless absolutely necessary. He also says the killer can easily be recognised as he has a hook in place of a hand. The young girl looks worriedly at her boyfriend and tells him she is scared and wants to go home. He calmly tells her there is nothing to be worried about, and besides, he is there to protect her. The girl calms down and they proceed to Lovers' Lane.

Just after they start getting amorous, the girl hears a rustling noise from the nearby woods and becomes petrified. She pleads with her boyfriend to take her home, but he is very reluctant and an argument ensues. The girl is so frantic that the boyfriend eventually gives in. The boyfriend turns the ignition key, and roars away down the lane in utter frustration.

After a journey in sulky silence, the young couple arrive at the girl's house. The boyfriend (even though mad with her, he hasn't forgotten his manners) gets out of the car and walks around the other side to open her door. He stops dead, turns as white as a ghost and faints. The girlfriend hurriedly gets out of the car to tend to him. As she shuts the car door behind her, she hears a 'clank' and turns around. There, swinging backwards and forwards is a bloody hook dangling on the door handle.

The Investigation

The Hook needs no introduction. If you have never heard this story, then I welcome you to our planet, and I hope you come in peace! This UL has been kicking around the campfires since at least the 1950s, although its origins are unclear. This story is particularly unnerving, as it conjures up disturbing thoughts of 'What if?' The teenage couple obviously escape with their lives at the last moment, and it is a chain of events that lead to their lucky escape. If the young girl had let her boyfriend get his own way and decided to stay, then they would not have escaped; likewise if the boyfriend hadn't been so annoyed and stepped on the accelerator, roaring off down the lane. This very action leads to the climax of the story, with the bloody hook left dangling on the door handle. This image is a realisation of what could have been.

And Finally...

I have defined this UL as 'undecided' because the basic outline could well have been based on true-life experiences. It is reported that Lovers' Lane murders did occur in the 1940s, but there are no records of murders committed by a man with a hook for a hand, so it is likely that the story has been embellished to increase its impact.

This UL gives a good dose of 1950s moral standards. This period saw the explosion of rock 'n' roll and, in its wake, teenage rebellion. This was the first time that a true generation gap was created, and parents treated rock 'n' roll as the new evil (even worse than Eminem). Teenage girls found a new confidence, and started to rebel against their parents' old-fashioned views. They started going out with boys more freely, and this was seen as a threat by their parents. That is why I believe ULs like this one were made up to warn teenage girls not to let their morals slip. After all, if the girl in this story had succumbed to her boyfriend's wishes, she would have paid with her life.

Name:	Knock, Knock, Knock
Code:	HR4703
Origin:	1960s, USA
Status:	False

UNCOVERED

The Legend: Version 1

A teenage couple are driving back home late one night along a lane through woodland, when the car runs out of petrol. The boyfriend pulls over into a lay-by and explains to the girlfriend that there is a petrol station only a couple of miles up the road, and if he runs he will be back in no time. The girlfriend, unconvinced, pleads with him not to leave her alone. The boyfriend tells her that if she is scared, she can hide under the blanket on the back seat. When he returns, he will knock on the roof three times. Under no circumstances is she to open the door if she hears any fewer or more than three knocks. The girlfriend agrees, and after her boyfriend leaves the car she climbs into the back seat.

Twenty minutes later she hears a knock on the roof. Then another one, and then a third. She is just about to get up when she hears another knock. Now petrified, she sinks back into the back seat pulling the blanket tight over her. Further knocks on the roof follow and the girl panics. She quickly climbs over into the driver's seat, turns the ignition on and goes to accelerate away. The car surges forward a couple of metres and then conks out. The girlfriend decides her only escape will be to make a run for it. She opens the door and glances back before making a dash for it, but what she sees makes her freeze in her tracks. There, hanging from a branch with a noose around his neck, is her boyfriend. He had been bound above the car, and the tapping noises on the roof were caused by him trying to keep his balance, just managing to reach the roof while standing on tiptoes. She had killed her boyfriend.

The Legend: Version 2

The first part of this version is exactly the same as Version 1, so we will pick up the story after the boyfriend has left the car to run down to the petrol station. His girlfriend has climbed into the back seat and pulled the blanket over her, waiting for the three knocks to signal his return.

Over half an hour passes and the girlfriend is feeling increasingly worried. All of a sudden she hears the knock on the roof, quickly followed by a second and then a third. She feels relieved that her boyfriend has returned, but before she has time to get up, she hears another two thuds on the roof. Remembering what her boyfriend told her about the three knocks, she is now petrified and pulls the blanket even further over her head.

After a couple of hours she drifts off to sleep, only to wake startled by flashlights shining through the windows, and the wailing of police sirens. She hears a police officer speaking through a megaphone ordering her out of the vehicle. He tells her to approach the police car rapidly and not to look back. The girl climbs out of the car and starts to run to where the officer is standing, but the temptation is too much and she glances back over her shoulder. There, on the roof of her car, stands a grinning man with fierce wild eyes. At first she doesn't notice what is in his hand, but she soon realises that he is holding her boyfriend's severed head by the hair.

The Investigation

Knock, Knock, Knock is also known as 'The Boyfriend's Death', and is strongly related to The Hook. In fact, some alternative endings to Version 2 have the maniac standing on the roof of her car with a hook for a hand, holding her boyfriend's severed head in the other hand. I believe that this UL has branched off from the original Hook legend, and over the years has gained its own identity. The main difference between the two ULs is that in The Hook it was a close shave. If they had delayed their exit slightly, then the lovers would have been brown bread. Instead, they just got away in the nick of time, and the surprise at the end was a realisation of this fact. In Knock, Knock, Knock they are not so lucky. The girlfriend loses her boyfriend, and the boyfriend loses his head. Version I gives a double turn of the knife: not only does the girl realise her boyfriend is dead, but she discovers she herself accidentally sealed his fate. As ULs go, not the happiest of endings.

And Finally...

There are so many different versions of this story, making it one of the most versatile ULs I know. In recent years this legend has become as popular, if not more so, than the original source (The Hook). The earliest known documented version is attributed to a freshman at the University of Kansas in 1964 by folklorist Daniel R. Barnes.

The popularity of this legend may be due to the fact that the core elements are fundamental to the horror genre. The format of a young couple alone in a place where they shouldn't be, and doing something they shouldn't be doing, is a key element of any horror movie. A gruesome ending is inevitable; we just don't know how it is going to happen till the end. This is what makes it so compelling.

Name:	The Vanishing Hitch-hiker
Code:	HR4704
Origin:	Unknown
Status:	Undecided

UNCOVERED

The Legend

A young doctor was driving back home from an evening out one Saturday night when he had to stop for traffic lights at a busy junction. As he looked over to the side of the road, he was surprised to see a very pretty young girl, dressed in a lovely evening gown, beckoning him for a lift. As he had his golf bag leaning on his front seat, the doctor motioned for the girl to climb in the back seat, which she did. Still astounded by her beauty, the doctor asked her, 'What on earth are you doing walking around here at this time of night?' The young girl simply replied, 'It's a long story. Can you please take me home?'

The doctor said that he would and asked her where she lived. The address was quite out of his way, but he agreed to take her home. The journey did not take as long as he had expected, and they spent most of the journey in silence. When the doctor arrived at the address she had given him, he turned around to tell her they had arrived; but she had vanished.

The doctor, now feeling confused and in a state of disbelief, knocked on the door of the house where the girl had told him she lived. A frail-looking man opened the door and the doctor tried to explain. 'I don't quite know how to tell you this; I gave a

29

young girl a lift and she told me she lived at this address. When I arrived…'

The old man raised his hand to signal to the doctor to stop talking, and spoke to him in a very direct but weary voice. 'The young girl was my daughter. She was killed in a car accident on her way back home after her prom night. This happened seven years ago today, and every year I meet a different gentleman and have the same conversation as I am having with you.'

The Investigation

It is widely believed by folklorists that The Vanishing Hitch-hiker is derived from old European supernatural folk legends and was spread to the USA by European immigrants who had started a new life in New York, with the earliest known versions dating back to the end of the nineteenth century.

It could even be said that there is a version in the most famous book of all time (no, no, I am not talking about a Harry Potter book, I mean the Bible.) You don't believe me? Well, if you think back to your glorious days of Sunday school, you may remember the story of the Ethiopian who picks up the apostle Philip in his chariot, and how the latter baptises the Ethiopian and then promptly disappears. (Acts 8: 26–39, New Testament). Not many ULs can stake a claim to being in the Bible.

In order to be believable, ULs must adapt to stay tuned with the different time periods in which it is being related. In the earliest versions known, the girl would disappear on horseback. As the centuries rolled on, the form of transport changed to the horse and wagon, and eventually to the car, as we know it today.

And Finally…

So what makes this UL so special that it has remained a popular story throughout the centuries? The main reason is that if you strip the story down to the bone, you are left with a classic ghost story. The fact that the ghost appears to be so realistic and actually speaks with the driver makes this UL even more disturbing. This isn't a *Scooby Doo* ghost, which ends up being the old professor with a sheet over his head. This is more like a ragged looking Bruce Willis with 'I see dead people' still ringing in his ear.

If you peel away the surface of this legend, it appears that the dead girl is lost between worlds and the scenario of the girl's fatal journey home that Saturday night years before is being replayed over and over again like a scratched record, with her final thought of getting home safely still haunting her.

Name:	**Bloody Mary**
Code:	HR4705
Origin:	Unknown
Status:	False

UNCOVERED

The Legend

A group of girls are having a sleepover, and sometime during the night they decide to take it in turns to tell each other ghost stories. By the time the storytelling reaches Anne's turn, all the girls are already feeling freaked out. After thinking hard, Anne decides to tell a story that her aunty used to tell her. The name of the story is Bloody Mary and it goes something like this:

Over one hundred years ago, a woman by the name of Mary Worth was lynched from her family home by an angry mob accusing her of witchcraft. She was tortured and then burned at the stake, an event which was witnessed by the whole village. As the burning flames engulfed her, she screamed out a curse damning the whole village.

It is said that the vengeful spirit of Mary Worth can be summoned by looking directly into a mirror after it is dark and with no lights on. After saying 'Bloody Mary' five times, her face will appear in the mirror and... well, no one knows.

After Anne has told her story, the girls are shocked into silence. After a short period they start giggling nervously and dare one another to go into the bathroom, turn out the lights, look into the mirror and say 'Bloody Mary' five times. Anne takes up the challenge and tells the girls that it was just a story and that she doesn't believe in Mary Worth anyway.

Anne enters the bathroom, and the girls hear her say 'Bloody Mary' five times. After the fifth time there is deadly silence, and the girls start knocking on the bathroom door asking Anne if she's all right. After a few minutes the door slowly opens and Anne appears in the doorway. She is visibly shaking and has gone as white as a ghost. She is clenching her fists so hard that she has drawn blood in the palms of her hand.

Anne has never been able to tell the girls or anyone else what actually happened in that bathroom.

The Investigation

A story to spice up any sleepover, don't you agree? An absolutely classic horror tale that has all the ingredients for a UL, with garnish sprinkled on top. The tale actually incorporates a story within a story, making it seem very real, and very disturbing. No doubt almost everyone reading this has been involved in a sleepover of some kind and can relate to the story. Who hasn't told scary stories, trying to spook each other once the lights have gone out?

The story that Anne told was different, though. Like playing with a Ouija board, innocent fun can turn dangerous. So why did Anne tempt fate by going into the bathroom and summoning the ghost of Mary Worth? It's the thrill of the dare, the excitement of facing the unknown.

The name of the spirit that is summoned varies from version to version; the following are the most popular:

Bloody Mary
Mary Worth
Hell Mary

Mary Worthington
Mary Whales
Mary Johnson
Mary Lou
Mary Jane
Kathy
Sally
Agnes
Bloody Bones
Svarte Madame
La Llorna
The Devil

The number of times that the name is chanted into the mirror also varies. One variation is that you begin by chanting the name in a whisper and raise your voice gradually after each chant. After the thirteenth chant Mary Worth appears in the mirror and slashes your face. Normally the chant is 'Bloody Mary', but it can also be 'I believe in Mary Worth' or 'Kathy, come out!'

And Finally...

The origins of this UL cannot be easily traced, although throughout the history of mythology mirrors have often been seen as a gateway to other dimensions. In the past, mirrors have traditionally been covered up after there has been a death in the house. This is so the spirit of the deceased cannot glimpse itself in a mirror, condemning it to haunt our world forever.

Another interesting cultural link to this UL is that in times past young girls used to carry out a similar ritual. After reciting a particular rhyme, an unmarried girl would look into a mirror to see the image of her future husband.

A further version of Bloody Mary has the spirit of Mary Worth walking along roadsides looking for her murdered children. If a car picks her up, she disappears before reaching her destination. This version bears a very strong similarity to The Vanishing Hitch-hiker and is probably linked in some way.

Name:	The Roommate's Death
Code:	HR4706
Origin:	1950s, USA
Status:	False

UNCOVERED

The Legend: Version 1

A girl at college returned to her dorm late one night to collect her books and some personal belongings, before returning to her boyfriend's dorm to stay the night. When she entered the room it was dark but, knowing that her roommate was sleeping, she didn't turn on the lights. She stumbled around in the dark, gathering her books, clothes and her toothbrush, before leaving quietly.

The next day she returned to the room, only to find it surrounded by police. An officer asked her if she was living there, to which she replied yes. He then asked her if she had returned to the dorm last night, to which she answered, 'Yes, but only for a few minutes.' The officer then told her that her roommate had been murdered, and asked the girl to step into the room.

As the girl walked into the bedroom, she froze with fright. On the wall, written in blood, was the following message:

'AREN'T YOU GLAD YOU DIDN'T TURN ON THE LIGHT?'

The Legend: Version 2

Two roommates in college were taking the same class and had an exam scheduled for the next afternoon. Despite being reminded of the importance of the exam by their teacher, Sarah had arranged to go out on a hot date with the college hunk, and had no intention of revising. Stacy, on the other hand, was a perfect student, and had organised all her notes ready for a night of heavy studying.

That evening, Sarah spent hours putting on her make-up while Stacy had already settled down with her books. The girls were very close and Stacy tried her hardest to persuade Sarah to stay in and revise, worried she would fail the course. Sarah would have none of it, her excuse being she would revise for the exam in the morning.

After her date, Sarah returned to the dorm around 2 a.m. As she entered her room, Sarah heard a muffled noise coming from Stacy's bed. She presumed Stacy was tossing and turning in her sleep, and crept past her bed without turning on the light, so as not to wake her.

Sarah woke up late the next morning and was surprised to see Stacy still lying in bed. As Sarah went over to wake her roommate, she was horrified to see that the covers of the bed were soaked with blood. She hurriedly pulled Stacy over so she was facing her and saw that her friend had been stabbed to death. Sarah stumbled backwards, deeply shocked, and fell to the floor. As she looked up, she saw the following message scrawled across the wall in blood: 'Aren't you glad you didn't turn on the light?'

The Investigation

These versions are sometimes named 'Aren't You Glad You Didn't Turn on the Light?' and are just two of many. The common factor in all the versions is that the murder is taking place right under the nose of the unsuspecting roommate, and the killer scrawling the message in blood on the wall rubs in this fact. If the girl had turned on the lights, she would have certainly been the next victim.

And Finally...

This is another UL from the 1950s, and again a popular one among colleges in the USA. As with most other teenage horrors, a moral message is embedded within the story. It could be a simple warning that danger can be lurking around any corner, and it pays to be careful. It can also be seen as a message to the girls on campus that they not only need to be responsible for themselves, but they must stick together and be responsible for each other as well. Either way, it's just another cautionary UL whipped up by extremely paranoid parents.

Name:	Lights Out
Code:	HR4707
Origin:	Early 1980s, USA
Status:	Undecided

UNCOVERED

The Legend: Version 1

The police are warning that 25 and 26 September will be the 'blood' initiation weekend for all gangs. All new gang members (new bloods) will cruise around in their cars at night with their headlights off. As part of their gang initiation, they have to shoot and kill every person in the first car that makes a courtesy flash to warn them that their lights are off.

The Legend: Version 2

Police departments across the USA are issuing the following warning to motorists when driving at night: If you see an oncoming car without its headlights on, do not flash your headlights at it under any circumstances. This may be part of an initiation game carried out by new gang members. If you flash at the car, you will become their new target. They will turn around and give chase to you, and as part of the initiation they will try and gun you down.

This is becoming a very serious matter, and we would like you to warn your friends and family. Please take heed!

The Investigation

This UL has had three main outbreaks; in the early 1980s, August 1993 and in 1997. The first main outbreak in the early 1980s originated in California, and the gang reportedly involved were the Hell's Angels, who would have been riding around on motorbikes rather than in cars. The UL spread slowly but with conviction. By 1984 the story had spread to Eugene, Oregon (USA) and the gangs involved were now supposed to be black and Hispanic street gangs targeting white people.

The second outbreak was in August 1993, and with the help of faxes and the newly realised medium of e-mails it was speedily circulated. This time it was a warning about the 'blood' initiation weekend on 25 and 26 of September (1993). Of course, no incident of this kind occurred on the given dates.

The Lights Out UL disappeared for a few years before resurfacing in 1998, bigger and bolder than ever. The new outbreak sent the USA into a frenzy, with government and city departments sending out official warnings of the danger. The warnings were quickly withdrawn, but the damage had already been done: unnecessary widespread panic had been caused (a bad day for their PR department).

And Finally...

The Lights Out legend is false, although a similar incident did occur in 1992, when Kelly Freed (from California, USA) was shot dead while a passenger in a car. The driver had made a hand signal to some youths travelling the opposite way without their headlights on. The hand sign was supposed to be a signal for them to turn their lights on, but it was perceived as a rude gesture, and the kids gave chase and fired shots into the car.

A believed copycat incident occurred in 1993, when a man named David Vargyas (from Ohio, USA) was shot and injured again while travelling as a passenger in a car. The driver had flashed his lights as a warning to a car travelling in the opposite direction without its headlights on. The car gave chase and three shots were fired, injuring Mr Vargyas.

Was this UL started as a hypothetical warning about the increasing problem of gang initiation activities? Or, like certain violent films, does it just exploit and incite this kind of mindless violence? Your call.

CATEGORY:
COMIC RELIEF

I thought that after the blood-curdling ULs of the last section, it was time to bring back some light-hearted humour into our lives. So come out from behind the sofa, and prepare yourself for some side-splitting exploits and more mishaps than in a *Carry On* film.

Humour is an aspect of the mind which sets us humans apart from animals. It is woven into the very fabric of society and can relieve tension in the darkest of hours.

OK. Here's one for you. What do you get if you cross a funny (joke) story with a narrator who believes it has actually happened? An urban legend. Not very funny, I know, but true, and is probably the best way to describe this category.

From the witty and brilliant College Letter to the uncomfortable and disturbingly funny story of a Parisian bellboy, we have a selection of ULs that cover a wide range of comedy styles – everything from satire to toilet humour. So sit back and relax, and let the madness commence.

> *'Laughter is the best medicine – unless you're diabetic, then insulin comes pretty high on the list'*
>
> Jasper Carrott, comedian

Name:	Fart in the Dark
Code:	CM1601
Origin:	Unknown
Status:	Undecided

UNCOVERED

The Legend

A man hurried back home from work one evening so he could celebrate his birthday with his wife. As he drove home he felt a bit bloated and uncomfortable, which he put down to the birthday drink he had at lunchtime with his workmates. Lager always gave him indigestion.

When he arrived home his wife was there to greet him, gave him a birthday kiss and wished him happy birthday. She then gave her husband a blindfold and asked him to put it on as she had a surprise, which he obligingly did. His wife then escorted him into the dining room of their house and sat him down. Just as she had done this the telephone rang and she asked him not to peep while she answered it.

Now feeling so bloated he thought he was going to burst, he couldn't hold it in much longer. As soon as he heard his wife leave the room, he decided to let rip and released the noisiest fart he had ever heard. Not only that, it stank like rotten eggs. Now feeling relieved, he leant slightly to one side and let out a few smaller ones, thinking to himself that it was lucky the telephone had rung.

After a few minutes, his wife came back into the room and asked him if he had peeped, to which he replied that he hadn't.

She then took his blindfold off, and twelve uncomfortable looking people around the table, all family and friends, shouted 'Surprise!'

The Investigation

This UL has gained popularity and has circulated on a grand scale with the use of faxes and e-mails, and has also cropped up in joke books. Although featured in the book *The Heart is a Lonely Hunter* by Carson McCullers in 1940, this UL's origins cannot be traced.

And Finally...

A funny yet believable story; I am sure everyone reading this has an embarrassing tale to tell, like farting loudly in a crowded lift or during school assembly.

Name:	The College Letter
Code:	CM1602
Origin:	1960s, USA
Status:	Undecided

UNCOVERED

The Legend

The following letter was sent by a girl in college to her parents:

Dear Mum and Dad,

I have been at college for four months now and I'm sorry that I haven't written to you until now. Before I begin to tell you all my news I think you had better sit down. In fact, please do not read on unless you are sitting down.

Things are much better at the moment. My fractured skull and concussion, caused by jumping out of a window to escape the fire in my dormitory that happened shortly after I arrived here, are almost healed now. I was only in hospital for two weeks and now my eyesight is almost back to normal and I only get the migraines once a day.

I was very lucky because a gas station attendant working opposite the dormitory witnessed the fire and saw me jump out of the window. In fact, he was the one who called the emergency services. He also came to see me in hospital, and kindly invited me to stay at his flat because the fire had gutted my dormitory and I was homeless. I say flat, but it is really just a room at basement level, quite cosy, though. He is a great lad and we have fallen deeply in love and plan to marry soon. We have not settled on the date yet, but it will be before my pregnancy becomes obvious.

I know that you will both be thrilled with the news of becoming grandparents and will give your grandchild all the care and attention you gave me when I was young. We would have married sooner but my boyfriend has a minor infection and unfortunately I have caught it from him, so we did not pass the premarital blood tests, but hopefully this will soon clear up with my daily dose of penicillin.

I just know that you will embrace him as a new member of our family. He is kind, astute and ambitious, although he hasn't received a 'formal' education. He is also of a different race, culture and religion to ours, and I am sure your broadmindedness will not allow you to be bothered by the fact that his skin is of a darker hue than ours. When you meet him, I am sure that you will love him as much as I do. You'll be pleased to know he has a good family background, as his father is very high up in the arms trade business in his home village in Africa.

Now I have grabbed your attention, I should point out that there was no dormitory fire; I have not suffered any injuries; I have not been in hospital; I am not engaged and do not even have a boyfriend. I am not pregnant and do not have syphilis. However, I did get a 'D' in sociology and an 'F' in science; and I just wanted you to see these grades in their proper perspective.

Your loving daughter,

Sarah

The Investigation

This letter is hugely popular on the UL circuit, and has to go down as one of my favourites. Although very funny, this letter intelligently plays on parents' fears and attitudes towards college life. The tables are cleverly turned to soften the impact of the real problems; bad grades.

This version of the letter is from 1968, and although there are many different versions, they all have the same structure – the main differences normally being the grades and the subjects which the girl is taking.

And Finally...

The truth of the letter is unknown, although it is popularly believed to have originated from the 1960s. This is when college life went through some radical changes, and rules on dormitory life became more lax, meaning students had more freedom.

A variation of this letter was circulated by e-mail in 1998. This version was notable because at the end of the letter it was signed 'Chelsea Clinton'.

Name:	The Parisian Bellboy
Code:	CM1603
Origin:	Unknown
Status:	Undecided

UNCOVERED

The Legend

An American family were on holiday travelling around Europe, and they stayed for a few days at a hotel in Paris. After spending the first day sightseeing, they returned wearily to their hotel room, only to find it had been broken into. After a frantic search to find out what had been taken, they realised with astonishment that nothing was missing. But, strangely, the spare camera had been taken out of its case and left on the bed, and all their toothbrushes were lying in the sink. The father reported the break-in to the hotel manager, and the family were relocated to another room. The manager gave his apologies and told them that the bellboy was seen leaving their room. He went on to explain that it had been the bellboy's last day and that he was probably trying to play a prank, got disturbed in the act and left the room.

The American family went on to enjoy the rest of their trip around Europe, and thought nothing more of the Paris incident until they got home. When their photos were developed, they looked at them in disgust. At least ten of the photos were of the bellboy taking pictures of himself in the bathroom mirror of the hotel room. In each photo he was naked, grinning, and had one of their toothbrushes rammed firmly up his bum.

The Investigation

This story is enough to make anyone cringe. I am sure I don't have to tell you that the American family must have cleaned their teeth with these toothbrushes throughout the whole trip, oblivious to where they had been. This story does have other versions, but they normally involve an American family, and the hotel is normally in Paris. Why Paris? I suppose the French are an easy target, with the stereotype of the people being unfriendly and having a low-tolerance attitude towards foreigners (especially Americans).

And Finally...

This UL is a typical 'happened to a friend of a friend' story, with most people believing it actually happened. Perhaps it did happen; it is certainly quite believable. Other versions of this UL have been set in the Rocky Mountains of Canada, and most recently the tale involved an American family holidaying in Mexico.

Name:	Stand-off at Sea
Code:	CM1604
Origin:	Unknown
Status:	False

UNCOVERED

The Legend

The following conversation took place between two radio operators at sea. Radio Operator One was aboard a US Navy ship.

Radio Operator One: Request that you change your course by 20 degrees to the north to prevent a collision.

Radio Operator Two: Request you change YOUR course by 20 degrees.

Radio Operator One: You are speaking to the captain of a US Navy ship. I repeat, change your course.

Radio Operator Two: No, recommend you divert YOUR course.

Radio Operator One: This is a large US Navy warship. Divert your course immediately!

Radio Operator Two: This is a lighthouse. Your call.

The Investigation

This UL, although false, is a story that the US Navy undoubtedly would like to shake off. This embarrassing tale was supposedly recorded by the Chief of Naval Operations in 1995, although the UL has been around for at least twenty years. The operator in the warship, with his arrogant, pompous and self-righteous attitude, is pleasingly outwitted by the matter-of-fact, deadpan lighthouse operator.

And Finally...

Although this UL is documented as being about twenty years old, many researchers believe it goes back a lot further than that. Copies of this story are believed to have been passed around the US Navy in the 1960s as a joke.

Name:	The Cat Flap
Code:	CM1605
Origin:	The Big Issue Magazine
Status:	False

UNCOVERED

The Legend

In Germany, a man named Gunther Burpus (41) of Bremen remained stuck in his cat flap for two days because passers-by thought it was a modern art exhibition.

After mislaying his keys, Mr Burpus decided he would try and reach the handle of the front door to the house via the cat flap. He managed to get his head and shoulders in the cat flap before realising he was completely wedged in. He called out for help, which attracted the attention of a group of youths. Instead of helping him, they pulled down his trousers and pants, before running off laughing. They returned shortly afterwards with a can of paint, and painted Mr Burpus's bottom bright blue. To add a finishing touch, they stuck a daffodil between his buttocks. Before leaving, the youths erected a sign reading 'An essay in street art – please give generously'.

Passers-by thought that Mr Burpus's screams for help was just an act and part of the exhibition. Mr Burpus was stuck in the cat flap for two days, and was only rescued by the police because an old lady complained after seeing a dog lick his private parts. Mr Burpus told the police that his cries for help were ignored, and that people threw spare change into the back of his trousers commenting on how fantastic the exhibition was.

The Investigation

This story originated from a copy of *The Big Issue*, a magazine in aid of homeless people, and spread quickly across the Internet, TV and the radio. Other magazines and newspapers also printed the story. The tale of Mr Burpus is false, as no record can be found of it actually happening. Even the German newspaper that supposedly reported the story had no record of it actually being printed.

And Finally...

This UL is funny and disturbing at the same time. It plays on a fear that everybody possesses: having to rely on the goodness of mankind when needing help in a serious situation. We would all like to think that if it came to it, strangers would offer us help if we needed it. In this story the opposite happened; and the passers-by were too ignorant or uncaring to realise that Mr Burpus really needed help. This UL pokes a sharp stick at modern society.

Name:	The Biscuit Barrel
Code:	CM1606
Origin:	1995
Status:	False

UNCOVERED

The Legend

One scorching hot day a woman pulled into a parking space outside the local supermarket. As she got out of her car, she noticed that a woman in the car next to hers was slumped over the steering wheel holding the back of her head. She felt concerned for the other woman, but carried on with her shopping regardless. One hour later she returned to the car, only to see that the woman was still in her car in the same position.

Now feeling very concerned, she went over to the car and tapped on the window, asking if the woman was all right. The woman in the car replied in a panic-stricken voice, 'Please call 999 – I have been shot and I can feel my brains coming out!'

The woman at the window noticed a grey substance oozing out between the woman's fingers from the back of her head. With this, she fumbled for her mobile phone in her handbag and called for help.

When the ambulance arrived the paramedics carefully prised the woman's fingers away from her head and examined the injury. Shortly afterwards, they burst out laughing. After they managed to regain control of themselves, they explained that the heat had caused a packet of biscuit dough (which was lying on the top of the shopping bag) to explode. The metal lid of the packet had struck the woman on the back of the head, and the dough had shot out and stuck to her hair.

The sales receipt for the woman's shopping showed that she had been sitting in that position for two hours before anyone offered to help. The manager of the supermarket gave her a new tin of biscuit dough.

The Investigation

This is yet another humorous UL that gives modern society a dig in the ribs. If this story was true, it is unbelievable that the woman could have been in the car that long before anyone bothered to help. Also, the fact that the woman assumed she had been inexplicably shot was a sign of the times we live in. On the other hand, it may have seemed very plausible at the time. She would have heard the biscuit tin explode and immediately felt the metal cap hit her on the back of her head. Her reaction would have been to put her hands to the back of her head, where she would have felt the warm dough oozing through her fingers and think it was her brains. However, it is not credible that after her initial shock the woman didn't realise that she hadn't in fact been shot, and that she then sat in the car for two hours.

And Finally...

The origin of this UL is very shady, although it became very popular in the USA in 1995. That year experienced a very long, hot summer, and during this time the story spiralled out of control. Although told as a true story, it became a popular joke circulating on the Internet. The story of a 'leaky brain' is nothing new, and this modern UL may be an offshoot of popular myths from days gone by. It even appears in the classic *Huckleberry Finn* by Mark Twain. Huck has a knob of butter hidden under his hat that begins to melt. When Aunt Sally notices this she says, 'He's got the brain fever as shore [sic] as you're born, and they're oozing out.'

Name:	The Bricklayer
Code:	CM1607
Origin:	1930s
Status:	Undecided

UNCOVERED

The Legend

A bricklayer working on a three-storey-high chimney had set up a pulley system so that he could raise the bricks up to where he was working. Although this was a good idea, he found pulling the bricks up in this manner too exhausting. Just then another contractor had some material delivered and it was placed on the roof by a forklift brought to unload it. The bricklayer seized the opportunity and managed to get the driver to lift the bricks up onto the roof as well.

After finishing the job he had a lot of bricks left over, and decided to use the pulley system to take them down. First, he climbed back down the ladder to the ground and attached a large metal bucket onto one end of the rope and raised the bucket up to the roof by pulling on the other end of the rope. Then he tied that end of the rope to a railing to keep it secure, and climbed back up to the roof. He loaded all the bricks into the bucket and climbed back down the ladder to the ground. He knew that the bricks would be heavy, so he wrapped the rope around his hand before untying it from the railing so it wouldn't fly out of his grasp. But he didn't realise just how heavy the bricks really were, and as soon as he had untied the rope gravity took over. The weight of the bucket was too much for the bricklayer and the force of its descent pulled his arm up so fiercely that he shot up into the air at high speed. As he sped up, he collided with the bucket of bricks that was now plummeting towards the ground, before continuing his journey upwards. Dazed, confused and with a broken shoulder, he hit his head on the pulley that was attached to the top of the roof. At that precise moment, the bucket of bricks hit the ground and the load spilled over. What goes up must come down, and with the bucket now empty, he fell back down towards the ground hitting the empty bucket en route as it was propelled upwards by his own weight. The bucket got wedged in-between his legs injuring his groin, and momentarily halting his descent. The bricklayer managed to struggle free and continued his fall. He landed on the pile of bricks that was scattered on the ground and broke his ankle. Although in great pain, he felt lucky to be alive. He freed the rope from his hand and cried out for help. Then, hearing a whizzing noise, he looked up – just in time to see the empty bucket plummeting towards him before it hit him on the head.

The Investigation

What a strange world we live in when we find such great pleasure in other people's misfortunes. It just goes to show that no matter how bad your day is, you know that somebody else has had it worse, and in a weird way that makes you feel better. But it's only funny as long as it doesn't happen to you.

You couldn't have had a much worse day than this particular bricklayer, although it was a basic mistake that led to the series of events. Instead of bringing the bricks down a little at a time, he thought he would defy logic and science and pull down a load that weighs more than his own body weight. I personally believe that if you are going to do a job, do it properly. Obviously a work ethic that this bricklayer has never heard of. If he had planned the job carefully and had the right tools and equipment he could have saved himself a trip to A&E.

And Finally...

This popular UL has been around for at least 70 years, as comedians have used the story since the 1930s. The Bricklayer has also popped up in many novels and films over the years.

Name:	The Naked Skier
Code:	CM1608
Origin:	1970s
Status:	Undecided

UNCOVERED

The Legend

A young married couple were on their first day of a skiing holiday in Austria. The girl had not gone to the toilet before they had left the hotel, and by the time she had got off the ski lift on top of the slope, she was absolutely bursting. Her husband suggested that she ski halfway down and relieve herself in the woods by the side of the slope, as no one would see her there.

The wife took up her husband's suggestion and skied down the slope and partially into the woods. She quickly pulled down her ski trousers and knickers and squatted. In her rush to relieve herself as quickly as possible so no one else would see, she forgot to position her skis in the stop position. Suddenly she started moving backwards and was unable to stop. She skied backwards and out of control through the trees and out onto the ski slope, picking up speed all the while. Down the slope she continued, with her trousers and pants still down by her ankles, and her bare bottom out on show for everyone to see. Still out of control, the woman collided with a post for the ski lift and injured her ankle. It was a few minutes before her husband skied down to her and pulled up her trousers to save her from even more embarrassment.

After reaching the hospital, the young woman started chatting to a man who was sitting next to her in the casualty ward. 'Why are you in here?' she asked.

The man replied, 'I was skiing down the slope, admiring the view, when all of a sudden a girl skiing backwards while pulling a moony sped past me. In shock, I lost control and crashed into a tree, breaking my arm.'

The Investigation

Another embarrassing tale of an unfortunate soul, this time caught out while on the piste. This is a very popular UL, and it is not hard to see why. This tale has the basic ingredient that all ULs must have; it's almost too good to be true. Although the 'humbug' part of you dismisses the truth of the story immediately, another part of you could quite easily see how it could happen. There are various versions of this UL, but the basic premise always remains the same. The location of the ski holiday depends on which side of the Atlantic the story is being told: the British versions are normally situated on mainland Europe, whereas the American versions tend to stick to the USA or Canada.

And Finally...

Still wearing its huge collars and flares, this UL has come strutting straight out of the 1970s. It is unclear where exactly this story originated from, as its popularity exploded in both America and Britain at the same time. Although the American version asserts that it was reported in a New Orleans newspaper, this never happened.

Name:	Take the Tube
Code:	CM1609
Origin:	Unknown
Status:	False

UNCOVERED

The Legend

A man working in a small office in the City of London felt very agitated when the large fluorescent tube which was lighting his office burnt out and needed changing. He immediately went down to the local electrical shop and bought a new one, replacing the burnt-out tube when he returned. Now that he could see what he was doing again, he worked hard to make up for lost time.

After a hard day slogging away, the man packed up and was ready for the journey home, when he suddenly remembered the old fluorescent tube. He decided to take it home with him, as he could throw it in a skip that a neighbour had loaned. So he started his journey home travelling on the London Underground. The carriage he boarded was packed, so the man had to stand, holding the tube vertically in front of him.

As the journey progressed, more and more commuters boarded the train. Thinking that the fluorescent tube was a pole to hold onto, people grasped it for balance. When it was the man's stop, several people still had hold of the tube, so he shrugged, let go, and stepped off the train.

The Investigation

This short and witty UL explains the way of modern city life in a
nutshell. The pace of life is fast, and individuality is sacrificed for
the soulless melting pot that is commonly known as the rat race.
People are too busy racing around from A to B to care about
anyone, or notice their surroundings. This selfish, unobservant
attitude is highlighted in this UL, with the commuters on the
Underground not noticing that they are actually holding a
fluorescent tube and not a pole. Although this version is situated
in London, it could have been any modern cosmopolitan city in
the world.

And Finally...

This is not a very well-known UL, and although it could take
place in almost any cosmopolitan city in the world, it doesn't
seem to travel well. It is believed to have originated in the USA,
and is seldom heard this side of the Atlantic. Ironically, though,
when I first heard this UL it was actually located in London, as
in the version given above. It was originally thought to have
appeared in a section of *Reader's Digest* called 'Life In These
United States', although that is not confirmed. The most popular
version of this tale is situated on the subway in Manhattan, New
York City.

Name:	The Unzipped Fly
Code:	CM1610
Origin:	1950s
Status:	False

UNCOVERED

The Legend: Version 1

A lady got in her car to do the weekly shopping but the car wouldn't start. Her husband told her to use his car, which she did, and he would have a go at fixing the problem. When she returned from the shopping trip she saw that her husband was working on her car. With just his legs protruding from underneath the car she thought that she would have a little fun with him. She bent down and unzipped his fly, slipped her hand in and gave a little squeeze. Giggling to herself, the lady entered her house and was horrified to see her husband sitting at the breakfast table reading a newspaper.

The lady stammered, 'Who's under my car?'

The husband explained that the problem was beyond his knowledge of cars and that he'd had to call the local mechanic.

When the lady had gathered her nerves, she explained to her husband the little prank she had pulled. They both went out into the drive and found the mechanic lying unconscious in a pool of blood underneath the car. The mechanic had hit his head on the underside of the car when he had reacted in shock to his fly being unzipped.

The lady dialled 999 and an ambulance was quick to arrive on the scene. The paramedics were carrying the mechanic on a stretcher back to the ambulance when one of them asked what had happened. When they were told the story they laughed so much that they dropped the stretcher and in the fall the mechanic broke his arm.

The Legend: Version 2

A young couple in Manchester were driving to the local supermarket when their car started juddering just as they entered the car park. The girl went into the supermarket while her boyfriend decided to try and fix the car. When the girl returned she saw that a small group of people had gathered around the car. When she got nearer she saw that a pair of male legs were protruding from under the chassis. Although the man was wearing shorts he was obviously not wearing any underwear as his bits were hanging loose for all to see. Feeling embarrassed for her boyfriend, she knelt down and tucked his private parts back into his shorts. When she stood up she found herself face to face with her boyfriend who was standing, watching, over the other side of the bonnet. The mechanic had to have five stitches in his head.

The Investigation

Version 1 is similar to the original versions that date back to the 1950s. Version 2, on the other hand, was found on the Internet in 2002 and is one of the later variants. These are only two of many, but can be considered a good representation of the basic story. Versions do not tend to differ too much, although the mechanic is sometimes swapped for a plumber working under a sink.

The Unzipped Fly is part of a larger collection of ULs that can be categorised as 'sexual embarrassments'. We often find this type of story hilarious and liberating as we can identify with the embarrassment but don't have to suffer it ourselves.

And Finally...

This UL is popular because of its simplicity. The role-play situations and the extent of the injury may differ, but the motifs of the legend remain consistent. Maybe another reason for this UL's popularity is that it is so plausible. And let's face it: if it wasn't for the mechanic's injury, it would have made his day.

CATEGORY: CRIME

After looking on the bright side of life, we turn our attention to the more sinister subject of crime. No matter what walk of life you come from, crime plays a dominant part in our everyday lives. With the technology of surveillance and security getting increasingly sophisticated, criminals are having to think of ingenious ways to beat the law. Of course, not all criminals are masterminds. Judging by some exploits, some of them must have thought God had said 'trains' when he/she was giving out brains, and asked for a slow one.

The following legends contain the good, the bad and the most unbelievable criminal capers.

Name:	The Sting
Code:	CR1701
Origin:	1950s
Status:	Undecided

UNCOVERED

The Legend

A friend of mine was driving home one evening when he decided to stop off at a shop and buy a newspaper. As he pulled up outside the shop, he noticed that he had parked on a double yellow line. Afraid of getting a parking fine, he decided to dart into the shop while leaving his hazard lights on and the engine still running, knowing that he would be quick. Not quick enough though, as my friend returned to find the car had been stolen. Realising he had also left his wallet in the glove box, he quickly informed the police and filed a report. He returned home late that evening and told his wife what had happened.

A couple of days later my friend left his house about to catch the bus to work, only to find the missing car sitting in the driveway. Astounded, he walked over to the car and noticed an envelope placed on the driver's seat. He opened the envelope and read the note inside:

Dear Sir,

I apologise from the bottom of my heart for taking your car. My wife went into labour and I panicked, stealing your car so I could take her to hospital. I know it was the wrong thing to do, and I would like to offer you the following as compensation for the inconvenience caused. Enclosed are four tickets to the FA Cup Final. The tickets are for the exclusive section, and are excellent seats. I hope you enjoy the game, and can find it in your heart to forgive me.

Being a huge football fan, my friend was very excited about the prospect of seeing the biggest match in the football calendar. He immediately ran back into his house to tell his wife and two sons that they were all going to see the FA Cup Final.

The day arrived and the family set off to see the match. After an exciting and thrilling game, the family got back home only to find that they had been robbed. The whole house was virtually empty.

They realised that they had been conned. The car thief had lured the family away from the house, knowing that they would be out all day. The thief had obtained my friend's address from his wallet left in the glove box. The wallet also contained photos of his two kids and his wife, so he knew that he had to get four tickets. The car thief guessed that they were all huge football fans from the football stickers and novelties in the car.

The Investigation

The theft of the car is purely opportunist, but the thief seizes on the chance to spin an elaborate sting on the poor unsuspecting family. The gullibility of the man in question is probably caused by the excitement of receiving the FA Cup Final tickets. Most people would no doubt smell a rat a mile off, but then again, any man who leaves his car running with his wallet inside is clearly wanting in the intelligence department.

And Finally...

Although the story seems quite incredible, it certainly could have happened. After all, professional con men make a living from the gullibility of human nature.

It is believed that this UL originated during the 1950s, and a version can be spotted in the 1997 film *Shooting Fish*.

Name:	The Body in the Bed
Code:	CR1702
Origin:	Early 1990s, USA
Status:	True

UNCOVERED

The Legend

A young couple checked into a prestigious hotel in Las Vegas. After entering the executive suite, they both noticed a putrid smell coming from their room. They immediately went down to the reception and demanded for their room to be cleaned. A maid was sent up to the suite while the couple enjoyed complimentary drinks at the hotel bar.

After the maid had finished, the couple went back to the suite only to find that the room still smelt foul. Again, the couple complained at reception, and again, housekeeping was notified. While the room was being cleaned for the second time, the young couple went for a walk along the strip.

After returning to their suite, they were immediately met by the same foul odour. Housekeeping was yet again called up to the room, and this time the couple went as well to investigate the source of the smell. They traced it back to the king-size bed, and to the mattress itself. After ripping open the mattress, they found the decomposing body of a man.

Apparently, the body belonged to a well-known gangster and playboy in Las Vegas. It is believed that he had been 'hit' because of a long-term feud between rival gangster families.

As part of an incentive to keep quiet about the whole affair, the management of the hotel offered the young couple complimentary stay in the hotel for life.

The Investigation

This legend first appeared in the early 1990s, and has many different versions. Yet all the versions have the same story structure and changes are only minor. Most versions are situated in Las Vegas, but the actual hotel name changes from story to story. I have deliberately omitted the hotel name from this version (I don't want to be sued!). Sometimes the victim is a prostitute and is found in a cut-out hollow under the bed.

This gruesome UL is told purely to shock. Las Vegas is a notorious haunt for gangsters, and the hotels seem a fitting location for such grizzly and shady criminal activities.

And Finally...

This UL is rated as true. Although a case like this has never been reported in Las Vegas, a spate of similar cases occurred across the USA in the mid 1990s, after the UL had become widespread. This suggests that they were copycat instances inspired by the UL.

The UL could have originated from a confirmed incident that happened in 1988 in a motel in Minneola, New York. The body of a girl was found in the bedspring of the bed after at least a couple of guests had stayed in the room and complained about the smell. The earliest reported incident of this kind dates back to 1982.

Name:	Grandma
Code:	CR1703
Origin:	World War Two, Europe
Status:	False

UNCOVERED

The Legend: Version 1

A family from London decided to drive to the south of France for a camping trip. Grandma wasn't feeling too well, and the rest of the family were apprehensive about taking her on the long drive with them. But Grandma ensured them all that she would be all right, and besides, she had been looking forward to the trip.

After the long journey, they finally arrived at their destination and began to set up the tents. Grandma had her own tent, while the rest of the family shared the other one. After a good night's sleep, the father entered Grandma's tent to wake her up. He quickly realised something was wrong and discovered that she had died during the night.

Now in shock, the family decided to cancel the rest of their trip and to drive back home immediately. After much discussion, the father decided that they would take Grandma back with them in the car. Having Grandma's body flown home separately would be too costly with too much paperwork involved. Besides, they were in a foreign country and believed the legal procedures would be too lengthy.

Grandma's body had stiffened and begun to smell, so they wrapped her body up in one of the tents and tied the package to the roof rack. When this had been done, they began their miserable journey home. The family were nervous about being stopped by customs. How would they explain having a dead body wrapped up on the roof rack? They had no need to worry. When they had crossed the Channel, they were allowed to drive straight through customs without being stopped.

Still a couple of hours away from home, they decided to stop for a break, and have something to drink and eat. They returned from the café only to find their car missing. It had been stolen along with Grandma.

They never saw their car or Grandma again.

The Legend: Version 2

A family were travelling by car across the Californian desert. The family consisted of the father, mother, two children and Grandma. During the journey Grandma fell very sick and within an hour had died. The father decided it would be too distressing for the kids to keep Grandma in the car, so he decided to wrap her up in a blanket and secure her to the roof rack.

After three hours of driving, they reached a small town on the outskirts of Arizona. The father pulled up into a petrol station, so he could use the phone to report Grandma's death and sort out some details. The rest of the family got out of the car to buy drinks and to stretch their legs.

When they all returned they found that the car had been stolen, along with Grandma strapped to the roof. Both the car and Grandma were never seen again.

Because there was no body to prove that Grandma had died, it took years for the insurance of her death to come through.

The Investigation

I have given two examples of this famous UL to illustrate the different perceptions of the legend depending on which country you heard it in. Version 1 is the British version, and concentrates on the difficulties of being in a foreign country under these circumstances. The family's main concern is to carry Grandma's body back to their homeland, without being stopped by French officials or British customs. This is because the family know too well all the red tape that would be involved if the death had been reported in France, let alone the time and cost involved.

Version 2 is the American version, and has a completely different outlook to the problems involved. The main reason for wrapping Grandma on the roof is not to upset the children. Also, as they are driving through a desert, I imagine the car would get very hot and Grandma's body might have started to smell offensively. The main difference between the two versions of the legend is that in the American version, worrying about crossing a border between countries and customs is not an issue. Furthermore, in this UL the disappearance of Grandma's body only seems to be a burden to the family because they are trying to claim her insurance money.

And Finally...

This is a modern-day adaptation of a UL that can be traced back to Europe during World War Two, possibly from tales of families attempting to cross occupied European borders to bury their deceased loved ones in their countries of origin.

Some folklorists believe that the legend goes back even further, with traditional old tales sharing similarities with this UL being traced back to the seventeenth and eighteenth centuries. Stories of thieves unwittingly stealing corpses, only to be shocked when they realise their mistake, have long featured in European folklore.

Name:	The Telephone Scam
Code:	CR1704
Origin:	Mid 1990s, USA
Status:	True

UNCOVERED

The Legend

A warning chain message was sent via e-mail and faxes, similar to the following:

Warning!

Con artists are phoning businesses and residents claiming to be BT service engineers. They claim to be testing your line and ask you to dial 90# (nine – zero – hash) on your telephone. Once you have dialled the numbers, the con artist has access to your phone line and is able to make long distance telephone calls that are then charged to your account.

This scam could cost you and your business thousands of pounds and needs to be taken seriously. Please inform colleagues, friends and family of this fraud.

If you receive such a call, ask the engineer for his name and a call back number. Then hang up. It is important to note that a telephone engineer would never ask a customer to help check a telephone line by dialling any numbers.

Please pass this information on.

The Investigation

Although I have marked this UL's status as 'True', there are some aspects that have been exaggerated. The main diversion from reality in the UL is that residential phone lines have never been affected by this scam. Telephone fraud of this kind is normally directed at businesses using networked PBX systems.

Also, the number that is dialled to give access to the line would vary depending on the PBX equipment that is being used. The con artist is simply gaining access to the outside line, so the number that needs to be dialled depends on what number your equipment uses to transfer the call for an outside line.

However, hustlers were using this scam to target London hotels in the mid '90s. Hotel operators were hastily informed of the scam and nipped it in the bud.

And Finally...

There have been other telephone scams, the latest being with mobile phones. Apparently, scammers found that if they dialled a certain code before dialling an actual telephone number, they received a free phone call. This is meant only for mobile phone technicians, who use the code to gain access to the line.

Name:	The Slasher Under the Car
Code:	CR1705
Origin:	1950s, USA
Status:	False

UNCOVERED

The Legend: Version 1

Last Christmas, a lady carried her shopping back to her car which was parked in a multi-storey car park. She placed her shopping on the ground and fumbled in her purse for the car key. Just as the lady had found her key, a man hiding underneath her car slashed both her ankles with a knife. The lady fell to the ground in such agony and shock, she was unable to scream. The man crawled swiftly out from under the car, grabbed her purse and shopping, and casually walked off.

The Legend: Version 2

As part of a gang initiation ritual, a woman's body part has to be collected and produced to the rest of the gang. The only rule is that this has to be carried out in a well-lit area. As this ritual normally happens at night, petrol stations are an obvious target. The assailant targets lone women and hides under their car when they are paying for their petrol. When the lone female comes back to her car, the attacker slashes her ankles with a knife. When she falls to the ground, the attacker cuts off a body part and runs off. The bigger the body part, the more recognition the gang member receives.

The Investigation

There are many different versions to this UL, and many are told as formal warnings. Version 1 is of the more traditional format, which has been told since the 1950s. Similar stories to this have been told in almost every mall in every state of America, all of them being told as an actual event that has happened. The story is very believable, as Christmas shoppers laden down with all the expensive gifts they have bought are vulnerable targets for muggers. This legend may have been originally used as a direct warning to women, to be vigilant when alone.

Version 2 has a more sinister undertone, with the threat of gang initiation rituals similar to that in Lights Out (HR4707). The threat of an attacker waiting for the lone woman to get back to her car is similar to the Back-seat Hitch-hiker (HR4701).

Both ULs have the same hidden moral agenda, raising questions about the vulnerability of lone women. This UL was born in a time when attitudes towards women were changing. No longer did women accept the role of the good little housewife whose only goal in life was to please her man. They wanted more freedom, to go out and enjoy themselves. Some people found this new attitude threatening, and it is possible these legends were used as scare tactics.

Time moves on, and the moral issues of the 1950s are no longer relevant. So the UL mutates with the changing times, and a new version is born (Version 2). This time it incorporates a different fear of modern society; mindless violence.

And Finally...

Although the first recorded case of The Slasher Under The Car was from the 1950s, the legend didn't hit its peak of popularity until the mid 1980s. Maybe this is because of the soaring crime rates in many US cities at the time, and this UL hit a chord with the justified fear and anxiety roused by the level of violence used by urban gangs and muggers.

Name:	The Supermarket Scam
Code:	CR1706
Origin:	Unkown
Status:	False

UNCOVERED

The Legend

A woman was carrying out her weekly shop in the local supermarket when she noticed an old lady staring at her. Wherever she moved in the shop, the old lady followed her. Feeling annoyed, the woman approached the old lady and told her to stop following her. The old lady apologised and sadly told the woman, 'You look so much like my daughter. Unfortunately she died a few months back, and I never got to say goodbye. I was too late arriving at the hospital, and she was already dead. I just wish I'd got to say goodbye!'

Now feeling awful for being so abrupt, the woman suggested that they carry on with their shopping together. The old lady thanked her, and told her she used to enjoy shopping with her daughter.

When they had finished their shopping, the old lady was first at the check-out till. As the shopping was being put through, she turned to the younger woman and said, 'You are kind like my daughter was, and have been such a comfort. When I leave could you say "Goodbye, Mum" to me? I think it would go a long way in easing my grieving.'

Although embarrassed by the request, the woman, couldn't find it in her heart to refuse. So when the old lady was leaving, the woman called 'Goodbye, Mum', and gave her a little wave.

When the younger woman's shopping was put through, the cost of the bill horrified her. Pointing to her one bag of shopping, she told the cashier there must have been a mistake. The cashier told the woman that her mother had said that she was paying for both shopping loads.

The woman ran out into the car park, just in time to see the old lady driving away and laughing out of the window.

The Investigation

This UL has many variants, but all carry the same message of mistrust. A person's good-hearted deed is always thrown back in their face, normally in the form of a bill. The locations of such scams do vary. Some versions are based in a roadside café, and normally involve a hitch-hiker getting stuck with the bill after being conned by a well-presented businessman who had picked him up. After lunch, the businessman informs the hitch-hiker he needs to fill his car up with petrol, and to wait here and finish his coffee. The businessman doesn't return and… well, you can guess the rest!

Versions that are located in a supermarket normally involve the same elaborate story used for the scam as in the above example. Quite often, the relative who has died is a son of the old lady and the victim is a man, but the same formula is used.

The way the scam plays on a person's good nature is seen as despicable by the listener/reader. This UL forces us to consider the depths some people will sink to just to get a free ride. Yet another satirical look at greed in modern society.

And Finally...

The popularity of this UL has gained momentum over the last decade, and familiarity with the tale is widespread across the world. Versions of the legend crept into comedy sketches and film scenes throughout the 1990s, the most famous being in the hit film *Dumb and Dumber*. More recently it has been used in the TV series *Hustle*.

Name:	Infected Needles
Code:	CR1707
Origin:	1930s, USA
Status:	False

UNCOVERED

The Legend: Version 1

During the school holidays, a group of girls went to see a film at their local cinema. When one of the girls sat down in her seat, she felt something sharp poking into her. She immediately jumped up and found a syringe placed in a fold in the seat. Tied to the end of the syringe was a note with this message written on it: 'WELCOME TO THE REAL WORLD'.

The girl was rushed to the nearest hospital, and the syringe was immediately taken away to be tested. The results were as the doctors had feared; the syringe needle was infected with HIV. Worryingly, this was not the first incident of its kind, and no doubt will not be the last. Please be extra careful before sitting down at the cinema.

The Legend: Version 2

Certain gangs are targeting clubbers with a unique and vicious hate campaign. Each member carries a wad of stickers, which are round, yellow, and bear the message 'Welcome to the Real World' written on them. The gang chooses its victims at random and, once selected, a member plants a sticker on the unaware clubber. The stickers are filled with minute needles infected with HIV.

Many incidents have happened at nightclubs and bars all over the country, and the victims do not know their assailants. Clubbers need to take extra care, especially when dancing within a crowded area.

The Investigation

The legend spans a timescale of at least 70 years. The original versions date back to the early 1930s, and are similar to Version 1. These early versions were also based in cinemas, with the only real difference being the reason behind the attack. In Version 1, the needle is maliciously left to deliberately infect a person with the deadly AIDS virus. AIDS was not known in the 1930s, so in the original telling of the tale there was another sinister reason for being jabbed with a needle. In 1930s New Orleans, young girls were warned to beware of the 'Needle Man'. Two men would sit either side of their young victim in the cinema; one man would then inject morphine into the young girl. Once the young girl was sedated, the two men would carry her out and she would be sold into slavery.

Version 1 originated from the late 1980s, when AIDS became a global epidemic. The media and governments around the world ran huge awareness campaigns to warn of the dangers of this killer disease. Of course, ULs thrive on paranoia, adapting to play on the fears of the time. Version 1 is probably a merger of two ULs: the original 1930s version (discussed above) and AIDS Mary, which will be discussed later.

Dance music exploded onto the scene in the 1990s, bringing with it the clubbing culture. Raves were rampant in Britain during the early 1990s, and drugs were closely associated with the phenomenon. Version 2 incorporates this new culture, and serves as a warning to clubbers to be careful. It also acts as a deterrent to keep people away from clubs. When this particular version was thriving during 1998, clubs were reporting a loss of revenue of up to 50 per cent.

These versions of the legend prosper because of the widespread fear of AIDS. The paranoia of the 1980s has died down, but everyone still knows the deadly danger of becoming HIV positive, and this ensures the UL's impact into the twenty-first century.

And Finally...

Although the status of the UL is false, similar incidents have occurred over the years. In 1989, a group of teenagers (mainly girls) went on a terror spree in New York City, jabbing pins into the necks of females at random. They attacked 41 women in this way before they were caught. The main concern was that the pins might have been infected with HIV, but it proved not to be the case. The gang's reason for doing this was that it was a bit of a laugh, just a game to them.

A similar incident happened on Rhode Island (US) in 1997. Two medical students jabbed 32 of their colleagues in the arm for a prank.

In 1999, a woman in Maryland (US) was attacked at a petrol station. A man approached her and demanded money. She told him that she only had a dollar. He told her that would do, put his arm around her and kissed her on the cheek. He then pricked her with a needle and said, 'Welcome to reality, you have HIV.' The woman was not infected.

A big problem nowadays is that robbers are using supposedly HIV-infected needles to threaten and rob people. In Britain this is such a problem that there are calls for the law to be changed, so that people convicted of these crimes will receive harsher penalties.

Name:	The Kidney Heist
Code:	CR1708
Origin:	1991, USA
Status:	False

UNCOVERED

The Legend

On a Friday evening after finishing work for the week, a man decided to go for a drink with some colleagues before heading off home. The man jumped on the Tube and crossed London from the City to the West End, and entered a bar in Soho. Not long after arriving at the bar, a beautiful girl started chatting to him. They seemed to hit it off and spent the whole evening drinking and chatting with each other. At the end of the evening the girl suggested that they go back to the hotel room where she was staying. The man couldn't believe his luck and promptly agreed.

After a short taxi ride they arrived at the hotel and went straight up to the girl's room. The girl poured a glass of wine for them both, and they both started to undress. Suddenly the man felt very drowsy and blacked out.

He awoke the next day in the bathtub of the hotel room, submerged in ice. He couldn't move and hurt all over. On the wall was a note which read, 'If you want to live, dial 999 immediately.' A phone had been placed on a stool next to the bathtub, within his reach. He dialled 999 as instructed and was put through to a paramedic. He explained his predicament and was asked if a tube had been inserted in his back. After feeling for it the man replied yes. The paramedic told the man to stay calm and perfectly still and that an ambulance was on its way.

The paramedic knew straight away what had taken place, as it was not the first time it had happened. One of the man's kidneys had been removed by a highly professional gang that specialised in the smuggling of human organs. The girl had lured him to the hotel room where she had drugged him; the rest of the gang had been lying in wait to perform the 'operation'.

The Investigation

This incredibly gruesome tale has been very popular since 1991, and has generated great interest from the media over the last decade. Stories of human organs being sold on the black market is nothing new, and the demand for them for medical research has led to some shady dealings in the past. I remember as a teenager reading about grave robbers that dug up dead bodies after they had been buried, and sold them to professors at universities for this very purpose. Perhaps the most famous instance of this was in Edinburgh, where bodies were reportedly stolen from Greyfriar's Kirkyard and smuggled through an underground tunnel to Surgeon's Hall. In Mary Shelley's *Frankenstein*, the monster was made up of stolen body parts and organs.

The difference with this legend is the fact that the man was still alive when his kidney was stolen. He was lured into a trap, and a gang that knew exactly what they were doing carried out the whole exercise. After all, it would take a skilled surgeon to perform such an operation.

The man was easy prey for the pretty girl… as all men are! In his desperation and lust he let all his defences down. This legend plays out a general uneasiness towards modern faceless cities, where you can't let your guard down for a second and you can't trust anyone. If you do, you could be the latest statistic on a crime sheet.

And Finally...

The latest versions of the legend differ from the original 1991 telling. In the original, the man was always with a group of male friends, being lured away by the girl. The bath of ice and the note did not exist back then, as the man normally awoke in a bed and manages to ring his friends, who rush round to his aid.

Although this legend is false, true stories of human organ thieving keep cropping up. Early in 2001, certain British hospitals were under scrutiny, accused of removing organs from young children and babies who had died, without the consent of relatives.

In India 1998, three surgeons and seven other people were arrested for unlawfully removing body organs from unsuspecting victims. The gang targeted the unemployed, offering them job opportunities. All they had to do was go for a medical. During the medical, surgeons would find a defect that required a minor operation. A kidney would be removed during this operation to be resold on the black market without the victim even knowing. No job was offered to the victim after the operation.

The outcry arising from this case caused the Indian government to toughen its laws, but still in some regions the sale of body organs is commonplace.

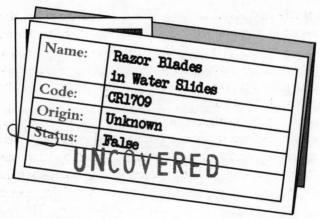

Name:	Razor Blades in Water Slides
Code:	CR1709
Origin:	Unknown
Status:	False

UNCOVERED

The Legend

A water park in Walton, Surrey (England) was all the rage when I was young, and the hot summer of 1985 was no exception. A water slide called the 'Black Hole' was everyone's favourite; a fast ride with an almost sheer drop in complete darkness.

However, during this particular summer, a certain story made people think twice about going there. Apparently, gangs of youths found it great fun to stop halfway down the slide and stick razor blades to the sides with chewing gum. A girl, aged 13, suffered serious injuries when her back and legs were cut due to the prank.

The story refused to die, and the water slide park's popularity steadily declined. The effect on business was devastating, and shortly afterwards the park closed up for good.

The Investigation

When I was younger this story was taken as gospel, and it did stop kids wanting to go to the water park. It was not until I read an article on the Internet that I realised it was a legend.

The article told about an event (similar to the version above) happening at an amusement park in Surfers Paradise, Australia. This supposedly happened in the late 1970s, and involved a girl (aged 12 or 13) being cut by a razor blade stuck to the slide with chewing gum. Versions of the UL can also be found in almost every state in America.

This UL is particularly malicious, as it has had an impact on the businesses involved. It is very believable that gangs would do this just for kicks, and the worrying thing is that the victim cannot do anything about it. The legend has strong impact because it makes people feel very vulnerable. You can travel down a water slide at great speed, and with little visual awareness. The feeling of being out of control adds to the buzz of the ride, but this very feeling fuels the fear that this legend generates.

And Finally...

An American version where the incident is said to have happened in England has an extra kick. It states that water slides are now banned in Britain because of the risk factor involved due to that particular incident. This is not true.

Name:	AIDS Mary
Code:	CR1710
Origin:	1986
Status:	False

UNCOVERED

The Legend

A bloke and his mates went out clubbing in Brighton for his twenty-first birthday. They were all having a good time and by the end of the night were all very drunk. When they left the nightclub, the mates sprung a surprise on the birthday boy; they had arranged a hotel room and a prostitute for him for the night.

Very grateful, the birthday boy staggered to the hotel and up to his room, where he met the prostitute, who was an extremely attractive young woman. After enjoying himself with her, he fell into a deep, drunken sleep. He slept so soundly, he didn't wake up till 11 o'clock the next morning. With a pulsing headache, he rolled over and realised the prostitute had already got up and left.

Still suffering from a hangover and rubbing his head, the young man staggered into the bathroom, and froze solid by what he saw. Written neatly in red lipstick across the bathroom mirror were the words 'WELCOME TO THE WORLD OF AIDS!'

The Investigation

This is obviously a cautionary tale and was first circulated during the AIDS frenzy and paranoia of 1986. As public awareness grew of the deadly disease during the 1980s, so did the paranoia on a larger scale. We have already covered these fears and anxieties of the disease in Infected Needles (CR1707). This is a UL warning of the dangers of indiscriminate sex and multiple sexual partners. The age of free sex that started in the swinging sixties was well and truly over. No longer could people have conscience-free, unprotected sex with just about anyone they wanted; they now had to think about the consequences.

This legend also tackles issues such as the danger and immorality of sleeping with prostitutes. The lady of the night in this legend obviously holds a grudge against men in general, whom she blames for her contracting the AIDS virus. She is seeking revenge without discrimination, and this unsuspecting man is the latest hapless victim.

There have been reports of similar real-life occurrences over the years. A British woman actually did contract the disease from her Greek lover while in Greece. The man, knowing he was HIV positive, had sexual intercourse with the woman without informing her of his condition. In North America, there have been cases of multiple people being infected by one person through sexual intercourse. Although it is not normally possible to prove if malice was involved, there has been at least one person (Pamela Wiser, Tennessee, USA) who has been convicted of this crime.

And Finally...

Another popular UL that is closely related to this one is AIDS Harry. This is a tale of similar theme, but the perpetrator is male. The legend normally tells of a holiday romance in a popular holiday destination such as Greece, where the men are reputedly very fond of British women. Just before the girl returns home, her male lover gives her a present; a souvenir of their romance. When the girl later opens the present, it is always something like a mug, with the words 'Welcome to the world of AIDS!' written on it.

CATEGORY: ANIMALS AND PESTS

Animals have always played a major part in all forms of mythology, legends and religion. A popular subject matter of ULs is snakes. The very word can make some people shudder, and they are often portrayed in mythology as evil and conniving creatures. The Christian story of the Garden of Eden shows the snake as the very symbol of evil and temptation, and they don't fare very well in the legend of St Patrick, where he was praised for ridding the whole of Ireland of these reptiles. Snakes in Greek mythology also have a rough ride, especially when famously acclaimed for giving the evil Medusa a bad hair day.

Not all mythology regards snakes as evil, and they were considered sacred in certain cultures. The Aztecs worshipped snakes, and the Aboriginals of Australia believed that a giant rainbow-coloured serpent was the creator of life. The rock python was considered sacred by some African peoples, and it was forbidden to kill any. Although snakes are regarded highly within these cultures and others, they sadly regain the 'Dr Evil' stereotype when it comes to ULs.

Another popular animal in mythology throughout the ages is the cat. The popular pet has had a varied reputation over the years that swings from one extreme to another. Cats were worshipped by the ancient Egyptians, and were supposed to protect the living and the dead from evil. They are considered wicked in other legends, however, especially when associated with witches and black magic.

Cat stories are very common in UL circles. There's a subsection of legends grouped together as the 'Dead Cat' stories. Cats are a versatile subject for legends, as typically they are either loved or loathed by humans.

Another form of cat legend is the 'Big Cat' sightings, which include snatched glimpses of animals such as pumas and panthers in urban areas. This topic is covered in the research of cryptozoology, which is the scientific study of hidden animals. I assure you I haven't made this term up; cryptozoology will be explained in greater detail in the summary of the UL The Surrey Puma (AN1602).

Finally, we have spiders. Spiders are a sure-fire fear factor, and our eight-legged nemeses are an essential ingredient in the world of ULs. These little creepy crawlies can strike terror in the hearts of the toughest of men, and transform them into snivelling babies. Go on, admit it – the mere sight of one in your bathtub can put you off your bubble bath for weeks.

Name:	The House Plant Guests
Code:	AN1601
Origin:	1970s, Britian/Scandinavia
Status:	False

UNCOVERED

The Legend: Version 1

A woman decided to buy a yucca plant to brighten up her lounge. She saw a nice one at the supermarket, and bought it while doing her weekly food shopping. After placing the yucca near the window in her lounge, the woman began to water it. Suddenly, she heard a squeak. The woman stepped back, wondering where the noise had come from. She heard it again, and this time she could tell it came directly from the plant itself.

The woman phoned the supermarket and explained about the noise. After being put on hold, a man came back on the line and gave her the telephone number for Kew Gardens, telling her to phone them immediately.

The woman didn't waste any time in phoning Kew Gardens. After explaining the situation again, she was informed that an expert was being sent round to her house. In the meantime, she was advised to vacate the house, taking any children and family pets with her.

One hour later, a white van pulled up sharply into her drive. A man promptly got out and asked to be let into the house. A few minutes later the man reappeared with the yucca plant and placed it into the back of the van, then quickly closed the doors.

Only then did the man explain what was going on. He told the woman that the squeaking noise that she had heard came from a tarantula that was nesting inside the yucca plant.

The Legend: Version 2

A lady brought a cactus home from the local nursery. She had only had it half an hour when she saw it move. At first she thought it must have been her imagination, but then she saw it move again.

When she reported it to the nursery, they at first thought she was deluded. Only after the manager had come onto the phone was she taken seriously. He said he would send an employee round immediately and told her to leave the house and wait outside.

The employee arrived promptly, and the lady showed him to where the cactus was. He was just about to approach the cactus when it suddenly exploded and baby tarantulas sprawled all over the carpet.

The Investigation

The popularity of imported plants such as cactus and yucca during the 1970s gave birth to this legend across Scandinavia and Britain. The British versions, such as The Spider In The Yucca, normally centre on the plant being bought at a brand-named store or supermarket. The versions told in and around London often state that an expert from Kew Gardens was sent to deal with the problem.

The American versions, such as The Spider In The Cactus, didn't appear on the scene until the late 1980s. These legends falsely claimed that the plants were bought at Frank's Nursery, a large nursery chain in America.

The American versions do not differ much from the European ones. Sometimes scorpions are found instead of tarantulas, and the ending is normally more dramatic (the plant explodes releasing hundreds of the baby creatures).

And Finally...

This UL may be 30 years old, but I hear new and different versions all the time. Only a couple of months ago it was reported in the local newspaper that a tarantula was found in a bunch of bananas bought from the local supermarket!

The House Plant Guests legends will spread and grow for many years due to one simple fact: the deep-rooted fear that many people have about creepy crawlies (especially spiders!).

Name:	The Surrey Puma
Code:	AN1602
Origin:	1959, Surrey (England)
Status:	Undecided

UNCOVERED

The Legend: Version 1

In August 1959, Mr A. Burningham was astounded as he was driving along a country lane in Crondall, Surrey one evening: less than 50 metres ahead of him, an enormous great cat the size of a Labrador dog was crossing the road. Mr Burningham pulled over and observed as the great cat crouched down among trees, watching lambs in the nearby field. After a while, the cat walked off out of sight. Mr Burningham continued his journey home, not quite believing what he had just seen.

In fact, it wasn't until there was another sighting three years later (1962) that he actually reported his own encounter. The second sighting happened near Farnham in Surrey, and was reported in the local newspaper. Ernest Jellett was walking along a country lane to work at the reservoir on the North Downs when he saw a big black cat bounding towards him chasing a rabbit. Mr Jellett shouted out at the cat in surprise and scared it off. The cat was described as having a round, flat face, a long thin tail and big paws.

The police investigated the story and found a flattened patch of ground where a large animal may have rested. The sightings continued throughout the 1960s, with big paw prints being found and strange howling noises heard at night.

The Legend: Version 2

The latest sighting of the Surrey Puma occurred in Guildford in October 2000, by Mr Quelsh. The large cat was spotted lying on a running track at the Spectrum (a sports and leisure complex in Guildford, Surrey), 100 yards from where Mr Quelsh was standing. Mr Quelsh commented, 'It was twice the length of a domestic cat and had its tail curled up above the ground. It definitely wasn't a dog, and did not seem aggressive. It lay on the green for a few minutes and then walked off into the trees.'

The Investigation

As you can see from the two examples, the Surrey Puma legend refuses to die. There are still sightings being recorded on a regular basis, 40 years on from the original. The first sighting was near the Surrey/Hampshire border, and most of the sightings since have occurred around the Guildford area, in such places as Cranleigh, Thursley, Godalming, and Guildford city itself.

Although the first sighting of the Surrey Puma was reported in 1962, it wasn't until 1964 that the legend really took off. Apart from weird howling noises heard at night, and big paw prints found across the county, other incidents also occurred. A flock of sheep stampeded out of a field, frightened by a strange animal. Nearby, a deer was found dead. Its body had been badly mauled and bitten. In 1966, a very blurred photo was taken supposedly of the Surrey Puma. The photo was so blurred it was hard to distinguish what animal it was, so can hardly be considered evidence.

The question is; if there is a puma roaming the Surrey countryside, how did it get there and why? Also, why has the animal not been caught after 40 years and how can it still be alive? Big cats can live to the age of 40, but it is unlikely that the sightings are of the same animal, which would imply that they are breeding. One of the theories of the origins of the Surrey Puma is that a puma owned by a well-known female singer was, at her own request, taken away in the early hours of the morning under the blanket of darkness and driven away in a horse box to be released into the woods.

Another theory is that domestic cats have been interbreeding with Scottish wild cats, creating a new species. Yet another wonderful theory is that the cats belong to a species that was supposed to be extinct. Big cats are known to have roamed Britain in prehistoric times – perhaps they never completely died out.

The most likely explanation is that people have illegally kept big cats then released them into the wild when they have grown too big or too much to handle.

Remember, big cats are for life, not just for Christmas.

And Finally...

The Surrey Puma was not the first out-of-place big cat sighting, and it certainly will not be the last. Big cat sightings are commonplace in American folklore, with stories of the 'Motown Panthers' being one example of many. Back in England we also have the 'Exmoor Beast' and the 'Shooter Hill Cheetah' of southeast London, which sparked the notorious 'cheetah hunt' of 1963. The first sighting of the cheetah was by a lorry driver, and the second sighting was by a police officer who claimed that the cheetah jumped onto the bonnet of his patrol car. The fact that a policeman reported the sighting gave it credibility and a huge hunt for the animal was arranged, involving the police and the army. Despite a comprehensive search, they failed to produce any trail of the animal. Scotland and Northern Ireland have also had their fair share of big cat sightings over the years.

Research into big cats is one of the many subjects under investigation by the study of cryptozoology. Cryptozoology is the scientific study and investigation of animal sightings that are unusual because of place and time, or when the evidence concerning an animal's existence is insufficient. Dr Bernard Heuvelmans, who was a scientist, writer, explorer and president of the International Society of Cryptozoology (ISC), first coined the term 'cryptozoology', and it simply means 'the scientific study of hidden animals'. The word is of Greek origin; 'kruptos' meaning 'hidden', 'zoon' meaning 'animal', and 'logos' meaning 'discourse'.

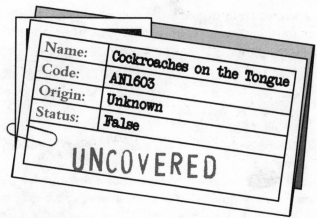

Name:	Cockroaches on the Tongue
Code:	AN1603
Origin:	Unknown
Status:	False

UNCOVERED

The Legend

In California, a lady cut her tongue while licking an envelope. At first she thought nothing of it, but after a week her tongue began to swell up. She went to see a doctor but he couldn't find anything wrong with her. After a few more days, her tongue had swollen up even more. It was now so painful that she had trouble eating. Her doctor sent her to hospital, and she had an X-ray taken to find the cause of the swelling. The doctors found a lump in her tongue, and decided to perform minor surgery. When her tongue was cut open, a small live cockroach crawled out.

After investigation, they determined that the envelope seal had cockroach eggs on it. The eggs were then embedded in the cut on the tongue. The eggs were able to hatch because of the lady's saliva, the conditions being warm and moist.

One Andy Hume is quoted on the Internet as saying: 'Hey, I used to work in an envelope factory. You wouldn't believe the things that float around in those gum applicator trays. I haven't licked an envelope for years.'

The Investigation

This revolting tale would make anyone think twice before licking another envelope, but the story has many flaws to its credibility. The main issue is that cockroaches do not lay their eggs in the way described. A cockroach carries its eggs around with it in a hard capsule called an ootheca. Cockroach eggs cannot survive outside of the ootheca. This fact alone blows any plausibility this UL had right out of the window.

Another question needs to be raised: is there such a person as Andy Hume who used to work in an envelope factory, and if so to whom did he make the quote? In the words of a famous rapper, 'Will the real Andy Hume please stand up?'

And Finally...

Although this UL does have an oral tradition, it has spread rapidly through the use of chain e-mails, and is firmly established in the cyber world of netlore.

Name:	The Log Flume Horror
Code:	AN1604
Origin:	Unknown
Status:	False

UNCOVERED

The Legend

A young couple boarded the log flume ride at a certain theme park in Florida. It was a sweltering day, and they both felt very hot and bothered after queuing for half an hour. Just as the ride started, the girlfriend suggested that her boyfriend put his wrists in the water; her mum had always told her to run cold water over her wrists to keep cool. The boyfriend shrugged and said that he would give it a go. But as soon as he put one arm in the water, he felt a sudden pain and pulled his arm out sharply. The boy was obviously in agony, and the girlfriend called out to stop the ride but to no avail. The boyfriend complained that his arm felt like it was burning and by the time the ride had finished, his arm was an unnatural colour, he had fallen unconscious and he was hardly breathing. He was rushed to the local hospital, but died on the way. It was quickly established that he had died from a snake bite, and an investigation was immediately carried out on the log flume ride. After it had been drained of all water, the investigators found the answer to the mystery. Near the starting point of the ride, they found a huge nest of water snakes.

The Investigation

The water snakes in this UL are often named as 'water moccasins' (or 'cottonmouths', as they are also known), water moccasins being the only venomous water snake. However, it is unlikely that this event ever took place as they do not form nests. They are solitary animals and do not live in colonies. They are not vicious, but would defend themselves violently if under threat. The venom from a water moccasin is not life-threatening and can easily be treated. Some people have been quoted saying that the bite is not much worse than a bee sting.

So, all these facts combined blast a hole in this UL big enough to drive a double-decker bus through. So why, then, does this UL continue to survive? Its survival is dependent on the fear of snakes. Throughout time, snakes have been cast as the evil villain in the screenplay that we call life. From Adam and Eve to *The Jungle Book*, snakes are sneaky spellbinding serpents that cunningly manipulate good intentions. They are seen as deadly predators, and can strike without warning and with great speed.

Snakes are the subject of many ULs, often similar to this version. Another popular UL involves a waterskier falling into a nest of water moccasins, with similar fatal results. Apparently snakes are also found on fairground rides, notably the tunnel of love and the merry-go-round. All the versions have one thing in common; the bite always results in a death.

And Finally...

It is almost impossible to trace the origins of this UL, although it was quite popular in some parts of the USA as far back as the late 1960s. This tale is one of many that fall under a certain category; a warning of dangers in so-called places of fun such as theme parks. Perhaps the reason behind these ULs is to warn us that the more we enjoy ourselves, the more we relax our guard, making us more vulnerable to dangers.

Name:	The Imported Snake
Code:	AN1605
Origin:	1968, USA
Status:	False

UNCOVERED

The Legend: Version 1

A woman shopping at a local discount store decided to buy a blanket that had caught her eye. As she put her hand into the fold of the blanket to feel the quality and texture of the fabric, she felt a sharp prick on her hand. Her arm immediately swelled up like a balloon and turned a deep shade of red. The woman stumbled backwards and collapsed on the floor. She was rushed to hospital but unfortunately died on the way.

When the police opened the blankets up, they found a nest of baby snakes hidden inside. An investigation found that the blankets were cheap imports from China.

The Legend: Version 2

A friend of my uncle's visited a large department store to buy a new coat. She tried on about a dozen coats, and none of them suited her. She was about to give up when another coat caught her eye – she just had to try it on. As soon as she had slipped her arm into the coat, she felt a sudden and sharp pain shoot up through her arm. She felt dizzy and collapsed on the floor; an ambulance was called. When the paramedics arrived, the lady was quickly diagnosed as suffering from snake bite. An investigation took place and two small snakes were found in the arm of the last coat that the lady had tried on. The coat had been imported from Korea. The lady has since recovered and is at present suing the store.

The Investigation

Born in 1968, this UL is a merger of two popular themes. The first one is the general mistrust of large retail establishments; especially budget department stores. Americans have always been wary of anything not made in the USA, and the influx of cheap imports from the Far East was seen by some as a threat to the American industries. The products are portrayed as of sub-standard quality, cheaply made and of mass production. The large retail establishments are the targets of these ULs, being accused of poor quality control.

The second popular theme is, of course, finding a dangerous animal in an urban environment. In this respect, the legend shares similarities to the Spiders In Plants legends (AN1601), and has been linked by *The Washington Star* (US newspaper) to earlier versions of The Log Flume Horror (AN1604).

This UL can be seen as a cautionary tale, teaching us to be aware at all times. Perhaps the message is intended as a blunt criticism of being 'cheap' and not buying good quality items.

Helped by heavy media coverage, the original Snake in the Blanket legend (Version 1) became widely known in the USA during 1968 and '69. Newspapers were running reports of supposed actual incidents, and most people believed the hype. Targeted department stores had to restore confidence among their customers by making formal statements denying that anything of this nature ever took place. Snakes were being 'found' in every garment imaginable, including rugs, rolls of carpets, blouses, jumpers and coats (as in Version 2). Then, strangely enough, the legend appeared to die a sudden death in the 1970s. As quickly as it had burst onto the scene, this UL almost disappeared in a wisp of smoke, but managed to claw its way back from the brink of extinction with a vengeance. In 1991 the legend was back, except this time it was only viper snakes in winter coats. The new target for the legend was a particular company (which will remain unnamed) famous the world over for its coats.

The victim in these legends is always a woman, and either dies from the snake bite, or recovers and sues the company involved. With regards the latter, normally the amount the victim is suing for is large and specified. The breed of snake varies with different versions of the UL, but in more recent accounts the snake is always a viper.

Some of the targeted companies of the legend complained of foul play by rival businesses, but this has never been proved and is unlikely. To spread specific rumours on this grand a scale would take a huge marketing coup of the unlikeliest kind, a flawless and untraceable smear campaign.

And Finally...

A bizarre and popular theory to the origins of the legend is the psychological link to the Vietnam War. It is believed that the legend was born in the late 1960s, with the fight against Communism in Vietnam in full flight. At this time, the American people felt total mistrust and fear for anything connected to the Far East.

Name:	The Dead Cat Package
Code:	AN1606
Origin:	At Least Since 1904
Status:	False

UNCOVERED

The Legend: Version 1

A young lady was living in a one-bedroom flat in the heart of the West End in London. The flat was small and the rent was extortionate, but it was close to the British Museum where she worked. Although she enjoyed the intense West End atmosphere, she still felt lonely as the cold, dark evenings drew in and winter approached. To combat the loneliness, the young lady's solution was to buy a pet cat.

The lady loved her cat, and all was well for a couple of years, until one grey morning when she found her cat had died in its sleep. The lady had no back garden and couldn't bear to throw the body of her beloved cat in the dustbin, so she decided to bury her cat in a pet cemetery. After making a few enquiries, she found out that the nearest pet cemetery was ten miles away.

The lady decided to make the journey by tube and set about getting ready. She carefully put the cat's body in a box and the box in a large shopping bag. The lady decided to stop off at a certain clothes shop en route, as she didn't normally travel that far and so hadn't visited this particular shop in a very long time. Whilst in the shop, she was looking at a couple of dresses and put the large bag down for a second. When she went to pick up the bag moments later, she found that it was missing.

Suddenly there was a lot of commotion just outside the shop. When the lady when to see what was happening, she saw that a woman had fainted and was out cold. Clutched to her chest was the lady's carrier bag, with the head of the dead cat protruding out the top. The woman was a known shoplifter who had been operating in that area for months.

The Legend: Version 2

Two old ladies were on their way to do some last minute Christmas shopping at their local shopping centre, when they accidentally ran over and killed a cat that had shot out in front of the car. The old lady who was driving was extremely distressed and couldn't leave the body of the cat on the roadside – she had to give it a decent burial. So she placed the dead cat in a spare bag and put it in the car, with the intention of burying the body in her back garden after the shopping trip.

After arriving at the shopping centre and parking the car, the two old ladies decided to have a cup of tea at the café to settle their nerves. Worried about the smell of the dead cat in the car, one of the ladies placed the bag outside by the front wheel.

The café overlooked the car park, and they could clearly see the car from where they were seated. While they were drinking their cups of tea, they saw a woman casually walk up to their car and pick up the bag. The woman then walked to the café and ordered herself a coffee. The two old ladies were shocked and slightly curious as to what would happen next. Sure enough, the woman slipped her hand into the bag to inspect her stolen goods, and with a loud shriek fainted and fell to the floor.

An ambulance was called, and the woman (who was still out cold) was taken away on a stretcher. Before she was placed in the ambulance, one of the ladies placed the bag across the woman's lap and told the paramedics, 'I think this belongs to her!'

The Investigation

This UL is typically moral-based with the 'what goes around comes around' principle ringing very true. The thief (and it is always a woman) always gets her just desserts for her ill deed. This UL also tackles the urban problem of disposing of the bodies of dead pets when you live in the city. Most flats do not have gardens, and yet you have to dispose of the body somehow.

In both Version 1 and Version 2, the dead cat is stolen by an opportunist thief, believing the package to be recently bought goods. Proving the familiar maxim that crime doesn't pay, the thieves get a little more than they bargained for. In other versions the package is not stolen deliberately, but simply gets mixed up with a similar package. The mix-up normally takes place on a form of transport, like a train, bus or ferry. The dead cat package usually gets swapped for a package containing meat; a joint of ham, for instance. In these legends, the reaction of the person who pulls out a dead cat instead of his/her dinner is always left to the imagination.

And Finally...

The Dead Cat Package legends are certainly not new kids on the block, and can be traced back almost 100 years. The earliest printed version was found in an article in *The New York Times* in 1904.

As Prof. Jan H. Brunvand once wrote, *'Never trust a dead cat story.'*

Name:	Alligators in the Sewer
Code:	AN1607
Origin:	1930s, New York
Status:	Undecided

UNCOVERED

The Legend: Version 1

In 1935, *The New York Times* ran a story about how a group of boys stumbled across something unexpected in the New York sewers. One boy was shovelling snow into an open manhole down East 123rd Street, Manhattan. Suddenly, he saw something moving directly beneath him. After a closer inspection, the boy jumped back and called over to his friends that he could see an alligator.

The boys managed to drag the alligator out into the open by throwing a lasso round its head, but the alligator had to be killed when it turned vicious. The article reported the reptile as being between seven and a half and eight feet long.

The Legend: Version 2

Florida, with its glorious beaches and sunny climate, is a popular holiday destination for Americans. During the 1930s, New Yorkers brought back baby alligators as souvenirs from the Everglades. Within a couple of weeks the baby alligators would grow quite large and become unmanageable as pets.

Some owners dumped the alligators in the street, but the preferred method by New Yorkers was to flush them down the toilet.

The alligators thrived in the moist conditions of the sewers, feeding on sewer rats and occasionally the odd sewer workman who was unlucky enough to stumble into their path. Because the alligators never saw the sunlight and lived in complete darkness, they evolved and became albinos.

The Investigation

The legend of the Alligators In The Sewer may have originated from *The New York Times* article. A further discussion point regarding the credibility of the legend can be found in a book written by a former New York City Commissioner of Sewers. In the book he claims that by the mid 1930s, there was a problem with alligators in the sewers. The problem was treated as serious, and another commissioner headed the investigation. He claimed that they did find alligators, but they only averaged about two feet in length. A campaign was immediately started to rid the Manhattan sewers of the reptiles, and in 1937 it was announced that all the alligators in the sewers had been exterminated.

These accounts may be convincing, but must not be taken as gospel. There may be grains of truth in the stories, but they may have been heavily exaggerated as well. Over the years the legend has grown in stature and popularity, with plausible theories on how the alligators got to be in the sewers in the first place and how they survived. It is true that Florida was already a popular holiday destination and is furthermore possible that baby alligators were brought back to the city as pets. But experts say it is impossible for the alligators to survive in the sewers for any great length of time. It is true that the sewers' water is a lot warmer than that of the rivers, but the toxic gases, hydrogen sulphide and the industrial chemical wastes that pervade the sewers would make the chances of survival minimal.

Another important aspect of the legend is the reproduction of the alligators over generations. Alligators nest in decaying vegetation and need the sun. The sex of the offspring depends on the temperature of the nest. If it is less than 86 degrees Fahrenheit, then the alligators will be female. The nest needs to be over 93 degrees for the alligators to be born male. (In between those two temperatures and the alligator could be born either sex.) So, as the temperature will always be less than 86 degrees in the sewers, none of the newborn alligators will be male. This would make it impossible for them to breed.

As the legend developed over the years, a common motif in the story was that the alligators' evolution turned them into albinos. It is actually very likely that the dark condition of the sewers would have made any alligators living there almost blind, and after generations would have turned them albino. Or perhaps their blindness is caused by their smoking too much of the white weed that is said to grow in the sewers, originating from all the marijuana that got flushed down the toilet during drug raids. But that's another story.

And Finally...

Perhaps these legends stem from the deep fascination and fear of what might be lurking underneath our cities. Is it really possible for such ferocious and dangerous predators to be hiding in the shadows of our cosmopolitan cities?

One theory is that this UL originated from an old Victorian legend about wild hogs living in the Hampstead sewers in London. It was rumoured that a pregnant pig accidentally entered the sewers through an opening and reared her offspring on sewer waste. These pigs were reported to be extremely vicious and could be seen occasionally emerging out of the sewers in Fleet-Ditch (Fleet Street).

Name:	Kaspar, The Wooden Cat
Code:	AN1608
Origin:	1926, The Savoy Hotel (London)
Status:	True

UNCOVERED

The Legend

Before leaving for South Africa in 1898, the diamond king Woolf Joel held a grand dinner party at the famous Savoy Hotel in London. Unfortunately, one of his guests cancelled at the last moment, which left a party of thirteen to sit at the table. A superstitious guest mentioned that it was unlucky to dine with thirteen people at the table, but everyone else just laughed it off. The dinner party was a success, and the host said his farewells before getting up from the table. Again, the guest warned him of the superstition, informing the host that whoever leaves the table first will be the first person to die. Woolf Joel, obviously not a superstitious man, found this hilarious and dismissed the idea before leaving. Within a few weeks, Woolf Joel was shot dead in his office in Johannesburg.

Fearful of any similar occurrences in the future, the Savoy Hotel management provided a member of staff to sit at the table with parties of thirteen. This proved to be unpopular with guests wanting to discuss private or personal matters, and so the hotel was forced to find another solution to the problem.

In 1926, Basil Ionides was commissioned to design a three-foot-high black wooden cat, which he carved out of a single piece of London plane. The cat was named Kaspar, and is still provided at parties as the fourteenth guest. Kaspar has each course served to him like any other guest at the table, even having a napkin tied around his wooden neck!

Winston Churchill was so fond of Kaspar he insisted that the wooden cat be present at every meeting of 'The Other Club', which has always been held at the Savoy Hotel. To this day, members of The Other Club have respected their founding member's wish, and Kaspar has attended every fortnightly meeting since 1927.

The Investigation

The superstitious fear of sitting thirteen people at the table may originate from Norse mythology. A legend tells of a banquet held in Valhalla, to which twelve gods had been invited. The evil spirit Loki gatecrashed the party and killed Balder, the favourite of the gods. As Loki brought the total number of the party up to thirteen, it is considered an unlucky number.

The number thirteen is also significant to Christians because it was the total number seated at the table for the Last Supper. Present at that meal was Jesus and his twelve disciples, one of which was the traitor Judas, who betrayed Jesus. Judas arrived at the table last, and so was the thirteenth member to join the party.

The story of Kaspar is an intriguing part of the Savoy Hotel's rich history. After five years' work and with great expense, the Savoy Hotel opened for the first time to much speculation on 6 August 1889. This grand hotel quickly established a reputation for elegance and style, boasting unheard-of features, such as full electrical lighting and 70 baths an unbelievable number for the time. Over the years, the guest list has read like a who's who of celebrities, politicians, writers, poets and the cream of high society. Lavish and extravagant parties were held at the hotel, one of which included a baby elephant as a showpiece.

The story of Woolf Joel's dinner party and his untimely death would have spread rapidly in high society circles, bringing with it new fears of the superstition. The Savoy Hotel's knee-jerk reaction of seating a member of staff at every table of thirteen was probably only partly to do with the superstition, and more to do with setting in place a damage-limitation exercise to restore their reputation.

Basil Ionides came from a family of Byzantine Greeks who immigrated to England around 1820, and became patrons of London's art world in the late nineteenth century. Basil had established himself as an architect and an art deco designer, designing many of the prestigious hotels, restaurants and theatres of the time.

So, I hear you ask, why a cat? Throughout the ages, cats have played an important role in many tales of mythology and superstition, and black cats are considered to be lucky omens.

And Finally...

If Kaspar could talk he would have a few stories to tell, since he was the VIP guest at all Winston Churchill's The Other Club meetings. Churchill jointly founded the club with F. E. Smith in 1910, with the idea of breaking down the barriers of politics, allowing figures throughout the political world to discuss and debate issues in a friendly and relaxed manner. The party was always served with exquisite cuisine, the finest wines and quality cigars; Churchill hardly missed a meeting.

Rumour has it Churchill was so fond of Kaspar that when two mischievous RAF personnel catnapped the wooden cat and flew him to Singapore during World War Two, Churchill ordered his immediate return!

Kaspar has also had a brief appearance in the harrowing novel '48, written by James Herbert.

The following selection of legends is not for the faint-hearted. Some of these ULs are bordering on the Classic Horror tag, but I have classified them simply as Horror for two reasons. Firstly, most of these ULs haven't been around long enough: in my opinion, a UL cannot be deemed a classic if it has only been around for a couple of years. Secondly, although these legends are immensely popular, they haven't quite reached cult status, which can only be judged by the number of variations and the importance of the role they have played at the time of narration.

The section begins with a proto-legend from down under, meaning it is a UL in the making. Whether it will eventually reach true UL status, only time will tell – perhaps I have helped it on its way by retelling the story in this book! Also included are such horror/slasher favourites as The Hairy-armed Hitch-hiker (HO4607), The Licked Hand (HO4603) and The Midnight Scream (HO4602), all of which give us pure horror stripped to the bone and in its most basic form, and survive and succeed because of their simplicity.

On the other end of the scale we have The Blair Witch Project (HO4608), a complex but manufactured UL designed to market a product. This is a good example of how a UL can be created to manipulate and control; in this case it was used to create hype to market a film. The potential for ULs to be used in this manner is something I will examine more closely later on.

I explore the fear of being buried alive (HO4605), as well as looking at the illegal and sinister trade of selling human flesh for consumption in Flesh For Sale (HO4606). Also included are a couple of ULs set on the original fright night, Halloween. At the same time every year these legends reappear on the scene, capturing the spirit of the occasion. The disturbing thing is one of these ULs is true.

Name:	The Dead Professor
Code:	H04601
Origin:	Australia
Status:	Undecided

UNCOVERED

The Legend

A female student taking English at Adelaide University, Australia was finishing off an assignment that had a deadline of 12 o'clock that night. By the time she had finished, she was running late and had to dash across campus in the pouring rain to hand her assignment in. The assignment completion box was outside the English department on the sixth floor of a building called the Napier Block. By the time she had reached the Napier Block, the girl was soaked to the skin.

While waiting for the lift to take her up to the sixth floor, she felt increasingly uneasy. The building seemed empty – even the cleaners had gone home. The Napier Block was in complete darkness. Although the girl knew that this was to be expected considering what time of night it was, she still couldn't help getting a little spooked.

When the student got out of the lift on the sixth floor, she failed to notice that a light was on in a room at the end of the corridor, about seven rooms away from where the assignment completion box was situated.

After handing in her assignment, the student pressed the button to call the lift. By the time it had come, she was shivering from the cold and just wanted to go to bed. Just as the lift doors opened, a professor came out of the room at the end of the corridor and turned the light out. When he saw the lift doors open, he ran down the corridor to catch the lift. The student saw him coming, and feeling scared, quickly closed the doors, shouting out: 'Sorry, you will have to take the next one.' She knew it was silly, but she felt very vulnerable and uneasy about the situation. The professor looked shocked and distressed. The student felt very guilty but put this out of her mind as she ran back across campus.

The next day, the student went back to the Napier Block to apologise to the professor and explain, but found his door still locked. When she went to the English department and asked where he was, they explained that he had died of a heart attack during the night. Apparently the heart attack was not a major one, but he had been unable to press the button to call the lift as he had collapsed on the floor. By the time he had been found by the cleaners in the morning, he was already dead.

It is said that when you catch the lifts in the Napier Block late at night, they will always take you to the sixth floor. Also, if you look in the mirrors at the back of the lift when the doors close, you will see the horrified face of the dead professor.

It is also rumoured that if you look at the Napier Block on a rainy night, at exactly 12 o'clock, the lights in the end room of the sixth floor flash on and off several times as the ghost of the professor vents his anger.

The Investigation

The origins of this proto-legend remain unclear, as I have only spotted it a couple of times on the Internet, both times written anonymously. I have e-mailed Adelaide University three or four times asking them if they could cast any light on the subject, but the legend seems shrouded in secrecy as I have had no replies. In one of the versions I read, it described the story as a local Adelaide legend. With this in mind, I have tried to contact various organisations within the Adelaide community, again with no results. It seems that no one wants to talk about this ghost story. How mysterious.

And Finally...

The Dead Professor is a typical campus horror story, similar to thousands of other legends told by students in universities across the world. Each university will own at least one legend that gets told throughout the campus year after year. This legend is not as widely circulated as some others, but can now be found on the Internet if you look hard enough, and the setting of this legend never varies from the Adelaide University campus.

On an Internet UL forum, a man calling himself 'Fuzzy' told me that he had studied at Adelaide University but didn't recall this UL. He told me that the English department is indeed on the fifth and sixth floors of the Napier building (which is often called 'the Napier Block' by its students). Fuzzy did find it strange that a completion time of 12 midnight would be given without the professor actually being at the completion box to see who handed their assignments in late.

Whatever the origins, this is simply a good old-fashioned ghost story.

Name:	The Midnight Scream
Code:	H04602
Origin:	USA
Status:	False

UNCOVERED

The Legend

In colleges across America, they used to have a rule of silence for a designated week to help students study for their exams. During these weeks in the 1960s a new craze was born called the Midnight Scream. At the stroke of midnight on a given day, all the students at every college would lean out their windows or rush outside, and scream their heads off for five minutes solid. This was said to have been a great stress relief.

During one particular Midnight Scream, a young female student was running down the fire exit staircase to join her friends outside for the traditional scream, when all of a sudden she was grabbed from behind. Her attacker dragged her down the remaining stairs and into a dark corner, and all the time the girl was screaming for help. Of course, her cries were in vain and lost in all the commotion. The next morning, the girl's mutilated body was found at the bottom of the stairwell.

Since then, every college in America has banned the Midnight Scream from taking place.

The Investigation

The strange custom of the Midnight Scream (also known as 'Primal Screams' or 'Door Slams') actually does take place at colleges in the USA. The screaming or slamming of doors is considered therapeutic for the students, who are under enormous pressure preparing for their final exams. The period of silence that is commonly known as the 'dead period' takes place just before the exams and is designed to help the students concentrate with their studies. In reality the 'dead period' can be anything from a day to a week long.

So far, so good, but at this point reality signs out and fiction clocks in. To the best of my knowledge and research, an incident like that detailed above has never happened. In some versions of this UL, the girl is raped and not murdered, but again, this is fiction and not reality. This legend, like so many others, was probably born out of the insecurity felt by students, caused by living away from home.

And Finally...

Although this legend can be classed as fiction, it may have roots in similar real-life cases. There have been many incidents where someone has been attacked and their cries for help have been ignored. Sometimes this is because of the 'cry wolf' syndrome, meaning in some urban areas screaming is heard quite often (typically just youths mucking around), so people fail to detect and react to a real and dangerous situation. Another reason may be that people are reluctant to intervene out of fear for their own safety, and for good reason as the papers seem to be full of stories of vicious attacks on 'have-a-go-heroes'.

Name:	The Licked Hand
Code:	H04603
Origin:	Unknown
Status:	False

UNCOVERED

The Legend

A young girl was left at home one night while her parents went out for a meal. As instructed, the girl went around the house closing and locking all the windows. She managed to lock every single window but for one, which was in the basement. She decided it would have to stay closed, as she wasn't tall enough to reach the window.

After having a shower and watching TV, the young girl decided to go to bed. Feeling a little uneasy about being in the house alone, she took her pet dog into the bedroom with her. As usual, the dog positioned itself under the bed, and the girl let her hand hang over the edge of the bed so the dog could lick her hand. She found this comforting and soon fell asleep.

Shortly into the night, the girl awoke to the sound of dripping from the bathroom. She was absolutely sure that she had turned the shower off properly earlier, and felt too scared to get out of bed. So she hung her arm over the bed for her dog to lick her hand, and promptly went back to sleep.

The approaching headlights of her parents' car woke the girl again a few hours later. Still hearing the dripping noise, she decided to go to the bathroom and make sure the shower was turned off properly. As soon as she opened the bathroom door, she froze in terror. Hanging by its collar over the shower curtain rail swung the mutilated body of her dog.

The girl rushed back to her room in panic, and cautiously looked under the bed to where her dog had been licking her hand. She found a note that had been written in neat handwriting simply stating: 'Humans can lick too, my dear.'

The Investigation

A version of this legend was printed in a book as part of a collection of modern fairy tales called *One Potato, Two Potato* by Mary and Herbert Knapp, in 1976. The version above closely resembles the one printed in that book, although there are many variations to this UL. In one version, there are two girls in the house alone. The ending is particularly gruesome as one of the girls cops it, along with her four-legged friend.

The unfortunate ending for the dog is a common motif in all versions of this legend, and the message left at the scene appears in most. Sometimes the message is written in the blood of the dog on the floor, and sometimes is worded, 'Humans can lick too, you know.'

In one version a slight twist is added with the story being staged at a girls' slumber party. The girl who is holding the slumber party is extremely snobby, and refuses to sleep in the same room as the other girls. She instead sleeps in her own bedroom with her pet dog. The story then follows the same formula as the other versions, except all her guests are slaughtered as well (and I don't mean drunk).

The Licked Hand observes a similar pattern to many other horror legends, most of which you will find in the Classic Horror section. Although the popularity of this UL is growing, it has not reached the cult status of some of the other horror legends from the same generation. The formula is the same used in slasher/ horror films, where the tales are normally 'no-brainers' and are gruesome and straight to the point. The intent is to make an immediate impact, using a chilling mixture of pure horror, revulsion and fear, with no use of psychological horror that inflicts fear through mind games. As with so many other legends, this may have arisen as a cautionary tale aimed at children. Perhaps the tale even originated with children, expressing their deep inner fear of being left alone at night.

And Finally...

This UL shares great similarities with The Roommate's Death (HR4706), especially as it includes a chilling message left at the scene by the intruder. In both ULs, the crime takes place right under the nose of the unsuspecting subjects, and this violation is brought to light by the mocking and terrifying message.

Name:	Buried Alive!
Code:	H04605
Origin:	Unknown
Status:	Undecided

UNCOVERED

The Legend

Many years ago, there was an old man who had been married to his wife for over fifty years, and loved her dearly. So when she died, he was absolutely devastated. In fact, he was positive she was still alive and had to be dragged away from her body when the doctor pronounced her dead.

At that time, a deceased body would not have been drained of any bodily fluids, and would have simply been placed in the coffin. It was also common for poor folk to have a burial plot in their back garden, as in this case. The old man still insisted his wife was not dead, and told the doctor that he knew his wife was still alive because he could still feel her presence. The old man became hysterical and had to be heavily sedated and put to bed while his wife was being buried.

That night the old man awoke with a vision so vividly horrific he couldn't stop screaming. The doctor was called, and the old man told him that in his vision his wife was still alive and was frantically clawing at the inside of the coffin. The old man was so certain of his vision that the doctor decided they would have to dig up the coffin just to put his mind at rest.

The next morning, the coffin was dug up and opened. When they opened the lid, they were met by a sight that would make your blood run cold. The old lady's face was distorted into an eternal scream, and her hands were facing upwards with the finger nails completely bent back. Scratch marks were clearly visible on the inside of the coffin lid. The poor woman had been buried alive.

The Investigation

The origin of this UL is unknown, but it is very likely that the legend originated from the paranoid fears of being buried alive that were rife in the eighteenth and nineteenth centuries. This common fear coincided with major breakthroughs in medical practices and techniques; one of these was the technique of resuscitation. Patients who would have been pronounced dead before could now be brought back to life. This newly blurred line between life and death caused panic among an often misinformed people. The thought of being declared dead when still alive plagued the minds of many. The so-called realisation that many people had been buried alive didn't help much either. Many of the coffins that had been dug up (normally by grave robbers) were found to have scratch marks or other disturbances inside. In those days, this was taken as proof of being buried alive; we know now of other explanations for this strange occurrence.

In those days, bodies were not embalmed before they were buried, and the bodies were placed into coffins soon after their death. It is believed that muscle contractions could move the body into different positions, which could cause the scratch marks on the inside of the coffin. Another explanation is the gas pressure inside the bodies; this could also cause the strange manoeuvres inside the coffins.

And Finally...

In the eighteenth and nineteenth centuries, the fear of being buried alive was so great that signalling devices for the coffins were common practice. These included placing a bell on top of the grave, with a pull rope run down into the coffin. Small flags or electric lights were also activated in this manner.

Name:	Flesh for Sale
Code:	H04606
Origin:	World War Two, Germany
Status:	Undecided

UNCOVERED

The Legend

The after-effects of World War Two plunged Germany into recession. During this time of desperation, money and food were short. At the same time, a strange tale was being spread by word of mouth through the streets of Berlin. It was said that a young woman had met and got chatting to a blind man at a rally, and at some point during the conversation he had asked her for a favour. The blind man wanted the young woman to deliver a letter to the house of a friend of his. The woman agreed, and took down the address of the house. She then became suspicious after crossing the street and looking back over her shoulder, when she observed the blind man scurrying away into the crowds without the aid of his stick. Instead of delivering the letter, the woman went straight to the police.

The police raided the address that the letter was supposed to have been delivered to, and found heaps of human flesh that were marked 'For Sale'. After opening the envelope, they found a note that read: 'This is the last one I am sending you today.'

The Investigation

I have not been able to prove if this elaborate tale is authentic, but what I have found out is that it could be based on elements of truth. The legend has a backdrop of post-war Berlin; Germany had just lost the war and the country was in turmoil. During these times work was scarce, and money even scarcer. It is possible that certain people would resort to cannibalism, and even capitalise on the situation by selling human flesh for consumption just to stay alive. It is also possible that this legend mutated from a piece of Nazi propaganda. During the war, rumours of Polish Jews killing young German girls for food were rife in Germany. Of course, there has been no evidence of such atrocities.

There is, however, enough evidence to suggest that the sinister trade of selling human flesh and organs does exist. One report I read was investigating life after Communism in the poverty-stricken ex-Soviet countries. There was one documented case from the Republic of Moldova, where a cleaner stole body parts that were ready for incineration and sold them to two local women. The women then cut up the body parts into steak-sized portions and sold them on the streets, selling them for half the usual price for meat of that size. One customer was suspicious, and the tests that followed proved that the meat was human. The Health Ministry launched an investigation.

Acts of desperation of this kind have also been reported in other suppressed and poor countries. It is believed that in North Korea human flesh can be bought openly at a farmers' market. Another disturbing belief is that orphans are sold on the black market to be used as food. Some people are cynical about these claims, believing them to be anti-Communist propaganda.

And Finally...

A piece of netlore spread around the web in the form of a disturbing e-mail, stating that the website Manbeef.com is marketing human flesh for human consumption. To protest, you put your name on the petition at the bottom of the e-mail and send it on.

Believe it or not, there is a website that has marketed gourmet cuts of butchered human meat. But reportedly this was only done as a hoax.

Unless you're Dr Hannibal Lecter, the thought of eating human flesh probably fills you with repulsion (although I believe it tastes like chicken!), and the thought of being tricked into eating it doesn't settle too well on the stomach. But what if you had to, like the survivors of the aircraft crash in the Andes (featured in the 1993 film *Alive*)? If you were starving and had nothing else to eat, would you? It's provocative issues like these that make tales of cannibalism so intriguing and such a successful topic for a UL.

Name:	The Hairy-armed Hitch-hiker
Code:	HO4607
Origin:	At Least Since 1836, Britian
Status:	Undecided

UNCOVERED

The Legend

As a woman was returning home in her car from a shopping trip, she noticed an old lady by the side of the road trying to thumb a lift, and obviously struggling with her shopping bag. Feeling pity for the old lady, the woman stopped and asked her if she would like a lift. The old lady gratefully accepted, and climbed into the car.

As the old lady got into the car, the young woman noticed that her passenger had large hairy wrists and arms, and was wearing a big chunky watch. Realising immediately that the old lady was in fact a man, the woman asked the hitch-hiker to check if the rear lights were working. As soon as the 'old lady' got out of the car, the woman quickly drove off and headed straight for the police station. When the police examined the bag that had been left behind, they discovered a sharp blood-stained axe.

The Investigation

This version of The Hairy-armed Hitch-hiker is typically British, and was popular in the late 1970s, at a time when people's fear and paranoia of strangers may have been heightened by the fact that the Yorkshire Ripper was still at large. However, the legend in fact goes back a lot further than that. The earliest record of this legend is a story printed in 1834 (in *The Stamford Mercury*), and another appeared in a book in 1956, titled *Negro Folktales in Michigan*.

In a modern time where hitchhiking has declined and is no longer seen as safe or socially acceptable, the UL has had to adapt. The popularity of the legend has crossed over the big pond to the States, with the modern versions based in a shopping mall car park. The locations of the mall differ from version to version, but usually a woman returns to her car from a shopping trip to find an old lady sitting in the back. The old lady apologises and explains that she was tired and just wanted a rest. The woman feels pity for the old lady until she notices her hairy arms; the rest you know. The only thing that niggles me about these versions is how the old lady got into the car in the first place – surely most people lock their doors.

Another interesting point is the rise in popularity of shopping malls as the location and backdrop of modern ULs. This trend is firmly rooted in the USA, where shopping malls have become a focal point of society. Not only are they a place for shopping, but also for meeting and socialising. Perhaps such legends as this one and The Slasher Under The Car (CR1705) tell of deep anxieties that something sinister could be bubbling under the surface of normality, and the shopping mall, considered by many as the safe haven of society, is no exception.

With this UL, as with so many others, the horror is what could have been and not what actually happened. We are given the tools, and it is our own imagination that is left to do the work.

And Finally...

Another narration of this UL, also set in a shopping mall car park, has a man offering help to a woman with a flat tyre. After the tyre has been changed, the helpful man asks if he can just have a lift to where his car is on the other side of the car park. The woman, feeling obliged, agrees. As soon as the man gets into her car, the woman feels very uneasy and makes an excuse about forgetting a shopping bag, hurries into the shopping mall and calls security. When the security man goes out to the car, the helpful man is nowhere in sight. He checks the car and finds a bag in the boot that contains a hunting knife and some rope. The man must have placed the bag in there when he was changing the tyre. Another twist to the story is that the flat tyre was perfectly OK; somebody had let the air out of the tyre. Instead of using a disguise, the man lures his victim into a trap by setting up a clever scenario.

Name:	The Blair Witch Project
Code:	HO4608
Origin:	1999
Status:	False

UNCOVERED

The Legend

In February 1785, Elly Kedward of Blair, Maryland was branded a witch and banished from the village after allegations of enticing children to her home in order to draw blood from them. By the following winter, nearly half of the village's children had disappeared, along with all of those who had accused her of witchcraft. The villagers fled in fear to escape the 'curse' that they believed had been put on them.

In November 1809, a fictional book called *The Blair Witch Cult* was published. It tells the story of a woman who, having been tortured and banished on charge of witchcraft, placed a curse on the village of Blair. This tattered book has survived but most of the pages are illegible.

In 1824, a new town named Burkittsville (population 194) was established where the village of Blair had once stood in Frederick County, Maryland, about one hour's drive from Washington DC.

Turbulent times followed for the townsfolk of Burkittsville, with a series of child murders and macabre occurrences taking place in and around the town. Perhaps the most horrific example was in 1941, when a man was convicted of the murder of seven children. He had disembowelled them in what appeared to be a ritual and claimed he had carried out the gruesome murders under the influence of the ghost of an old woman who dwelt near the woods of his house.

In 1994, three student filmmakers arrived in Burkittsville. They were collecting information for their class project on the Blair Witch legend and, having interviewed the townsfolk, they set off into the nearby woods to gather footage for their film, never to be seen again.

A huge operation to find the students ensued, but after ten days of combing the woodlands with the aid of tracking dogs, helicopters and even a department of defence satellite, the rescuers returned unsuccessful.

For a year their disappearance remained a mystery, until the film footage they had shot was discovered buried under an old log cabin in the woods.

The Investigation

The Blair Witch Project was groundbreaking, as it was the first time that a UL was created with the sole purpose of marketing a film. This low-budget production used the power of ULs to maximum effect and, in doing so, achieved massive publicity before the film was even released. The Blair Witch website supplies a formidable and extremely detailed history of the legend, giving a credible background to the film. The film itself is said to be the actual footage filmed by the students, shortly before they disappeared. The footage was found a year after their disappearance in an abandoned log cabin, and was titled *The Blair Witch Project*. The whole set-up was very believable, and instantly gave the film a cult status before it was even released. Of course, we all know now that the whole legend is an elaborate piece of fiction, a clever piece of marketing that was the brainchild of the film's writer/directors, Daniel Myrick and

Eduardo Sanchez. Without a big budget to spend on advertising, they utilised the Internet to spin a unique piece of netlore; and it worked.

The film itself was produced in a unique way, and unknown actors were used to play the characters. The outline of the film and the characters' roles were explained to the actors, and then they were dumped in the middle of the woods not knowing what was going to happen. Notes and supplies were left in strategic positions for them, and they were monitored by a Global Positioning System that helped keep track of where they were. The end result was unique film footage that has a home video documentary feel to it, where the emotions of true fear and horror can be seen quite clearly on the young actors' faces.

In truth, the film never actually lived up to the hype, although it did prove to be a popular topic for discussion due to the fact that public opinion was so vigorously divided. The infamous shaky camcorder footage has not proved to be everyone's cup of tea, but was essential to get that student home video feel that the film relies on.

And Finally...

The Blair Witch Project reportedly took a total of $240.5 million at the box office, and $140.5 million of that was from the USA alone. To put these figures into perspective, you have to remember that the film was made with hardly any budget. It was one of the great successes of 1999, rated fourteenth in that year's top grossing films. It even beat off big-budget blockbusters, with films such as Wild Wild West, American Pie, End of Days, Entrapment and Big Daddy all finishing in lower positions.

Name:	The Halloween Horror Prediction
Code:	H04609
Origin:	At Least Since 1968, USA
Status:	False

UNCOVERED

The Legend

A famous psychic on a top US television talk show has predicted that a mass murder is going to take place at a college campus this Halloween. The prediction is that the murders will take place in a city that begins with the letter 'W', and at a dormitory that is 'H'-shaped. The dormitory is also situated near water, probably a small lake. The number of victims will be ten, and they will all be female students. The killer will be wearing a '*Scream*' mask, and the murder weapon is a hatchet.

The Investigation

The TV talk show that the psychic is supposed to have appeared on is normally stated, and in recent versions is usually hosted by Oprah Winfrey or Montel Williams. The fact that no one has ever seen this particular show is sometimes explained by stating that the show was taped but never aired.

In the latest versions, the killer is said to be wearing a '*Scream*' mask (as in Edvard Munch's famous painting, made even more famous by the recent slasher movies). In the earlier versions (pre

1998), the killer was said to be dressed up as Little Bo Peep. The weapon of choice varies from version to version, but is usually a sharp instrument like a knife, hatchet or axe. The number of victims also varies, but is usually one of the following numbers: 9, 10, 12, 15 or 18.

The location of the campus is normally explained in a cryptic prediction. For instance, the campus is in a city that begins with the letter 'M' or 'W', and is adjacent to a cemetery, rail track, etc.

As with other campus legends, such as The Midnight Scream (HO4602) and The Roommate's Death (HR4706), the Halloween Horror Prediction exploits the sense of insecurity about dormitory life on campus. This is explained in greater detail in the 'And Finally...' part of The College Letter (CM1602).

Although the rumours seem highly implausible, the threat was considered serious enough at some universities for them to ban Little Bo Peep costumes at their Halloween parties.

And Finally...

This UL has been around since at least 1968, where similar rumours were afoot in the eastern and Midwestern universities of the USA. It was said that Jean Dixon had predicted the murders on a radio program.

The legend has had spurts of popularity in the following years: 1968, '79, '83, '86, '88, '91 and '98. The sudden popularity of the UL in 1998, and of horror legends in general around this time, has been heavily associated with the success of the film *Urban Legends*, which was released that same year in the cinema.

Name:	Trick in Treats
Code:	HO4610
Origin:	USA
Status:	True

UNCOVERED

The Legend

WARNING!

Every year at Halloween, kids dress up in ghoulish costumes and go trick-or-treating. This is seen as harmless fun by many and is usually carried out under adult supervision. The reason why this exercise is called 'trick-or-treat' is simple, the kids knock on a door and when a person answers they are asked a simple question: 'Trick or treat?' The person then has to give the trick-or-treaters a treat (e.g. sweets, chocolate, apples, etc.), or pay the penalty with a trick. The trick is usually a practical joke with no malice involved, although some kids may take this a bit too far.

This custom has been carried out for generations, and so it is a sign of the times when parents have to be careful about the treats the kids are receiving. I am afraid there are some truly wicked and twisted people out there, who seem to take great pleasure in tampering with the kids' treats. In some of the most serious cases, razor blades and pins have been found embedded in apples. It is only a matter of time before serious injury is caused by such callous acts.

So, I ask all parents to be extremely vigilant and not allow your children to go trick-or-treating without adult supervision. Always check the treats for signs of tampering, and especially be wary of anything homemade (e.g. cakes).

Happy trick-or-treating!

The Investigation

It seems unbelievable but it's true – these depraved individuals who interfere with kids' treats really do exist. The warning above is typical of many that appear in e-mail in-trays or through fax machines just before Halloween every year. It is a warning with basis, and should never go unheeded. Over the years there have been many incidences of this kind of food tampering, and the threat has prompted official warnings to be issued. In 1997, the CPSC (Consumer Product Safety Commission) issued the following safety tip for Halloween trick-or-treating: 'Warn children not to eat any treats before an adult has examined them carefully for evidence of tampering.'

Although still a threat, the stories have turned into legends over the years and are often greatly exaggerated. Most cases reported have turned out to be hoaxes and out of the incidents that have actually happened, luckily no one has been seriously injured. The stories started to fly around in the late sixties, and the number of incidents reached a record high in 1982. In this particular year, there was an influx of food tampering instances, and not just over the period of Halloween.

Although hugely popular in the USA, trick-or-treating in Britain was almost unheard of before the 1980s. When the US custom did take off in Britain in the mid 1980s, so did all the legends that went with it. British parents were particularly cautious about their children going trick-or-treating, on hearing all at once a plethora of stories about food tampering, poisoning and kidnapping. Many households banned trick-or-treating, and trick-or-treaters were shown hostility. Of course, the media gave more than a helping hand to whip up the frenzy.

And Finally...

The modern practice of trick-or-treating probably originated from a Celtic New Year tradition of placing treats on the doorstep for the spirits that haunted the night, looking for people to possess. The idea was that the treats would please the spirits, and so these would leave the occupants of the house in peace.

Christians had a similar ritual called 'souling', which would take place on 2 November around the ninth century AD. A participant would knock on doors, and the person who answered the door would exchange 'soul cakes' (square pieces of bread with currants) for a prayer for deceased relatives. The more cakes that were given, the more prayers would be said, increasing the chances that the deceased relative's soul would find heaven.

CATEGORY:
TRAINS, PLANES AND AUTOMOBILES

Mankind has never quite grasped the concept of adapting to the environment; it is more a case of adapting the environment to suit mankind. Never being satisfied with just our own two feet, we have always contrived different ways to help us get from A to B that little bit faster. From the invention of the wheel it has been an epic journey of discovery that can only be described as an obsession. The last century saw technology finally keeping up with our dreams, and the possibilities of travel suddenly seemed limitless. From flying across the Atlantic and exploring space to reaching the deepest depths of our oceans and flying supersonic, the boundaries have been pushed back further and further.

Out of all the modes of transport that we have in the modern world, the motorcar has been the one that has affected us the most. We simply could not live without them these days and we cannot imagine what life was like before them. Although most of us will not go as far as one American from one of those sunny states down south, who was so fanatical about his car that he actually married it, it is safe to say that the UK is a nation obsessed with cars. The back catalogue of ULs about cars is huge, and they range from the cheeky The Clever Motorist (TR8712), to the sinister Ghostly Handprints (TR8702), to the downright stupid The JATO Rocket Car (TR8711). Just for good measure we also touch on the present day traffic hysteria known as road rage with Battle Of The Ages (TR8705) and The Road Hog (TR8704), while discussing the reasons why you are not allowed to use mobile phones at petrol stations in TR8701.

Another of mankind's obsessions since year dot is the fantasy of flying. The Wright brothers gave us that dream, and it has been realised on a grand scale with commercial air travel. The airline industry is very demanding and cut-throat, but also close-knit, with many ULs developing from in-house jokes such as Mr Gay (TR8706) and The Locked-out Pilot (TR8707). Another legend, The Wooden Airfield (TR8714), is a great example of wartime propaganda, and it shows how ULs can be skilfully manipulated to serve a certain purpose.

The English are not a nation that likes to complain – in most situations we are more likely to grin and bear it, keep the stiff upper lip and all that. But sometimes when certain public transport standards are not met we feel it necessary to put pen to paper and write a letter of complaint. Normally you would receive a very apologetic letter back in return. Everything is fine, you have made your point and they stand corrected… unless the true feelings of the company involved are accidentally discovered, as in The Bedbug Letter (TR8709).

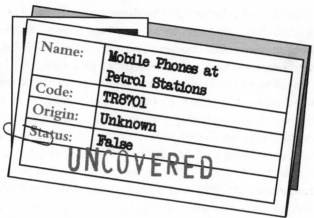

Name:	Mobile Phones at Petrol Stations
Code:	TR8701
Origin:	Unknown
Status:	False

UNCOVERED

The Legend

WARNING – DO NOT USE MOBILE PHONES AT PETROL STATIONS

A driver has suffered serious burns and his car was severely damaged, when his mobile phone ignited petrol fumes, causing an explosion. He was using his mobile phone while filling his car up when the explosion happened. All electronic equipment at petrol stations is fitted with explosive containment devices for safety measures but, of course, mobile phones are not.

Please read your handbook carefully, as all mobile manufacturers stress caution about using mobile phones at petrol stations.

The Investigation

Although I have rated this UL as 'False', mobile phones are considered a health risk at petrol stations. There has never been an explosion caused by the use of a mobile phone at a petrol station to date, and an explosion cannot be caused by the radio signals transmitted by mobiles igniting petrol fumes. The actual risk is if the phone's battery drops onto the forecourt; the battery contacts may momentarily short, creating a spark that could ignite flammable vapours. This risk is not only associated with mobile phones, but also with other electronic equipment that are battery operated, such as walkmans and torches.

The chance of this actually happening is about as likely as Bolton winning the Premiership, but the threat is taken very seriously. In Great Britain, mobile phones are not allowed on petrol forecourts under the conditions of the Petroleum Consultation Act 1928. The person with the phone cannot be held responsible; all responsibility rests with the forecourt owner, which is why petrol stations are so strict about the use of mobile phones on their forecourts.

And Finally...

These 'warning e-mails' exploded onto the scene in 1999, and normally referred to an incident that was supposed to have happened in Indonesia and, more recently, Australia. Investigations have found these reports to be unfounded, and an explosion at a petrol station in Australia was not caused by the use of a mobile phone, as many believe, but by static igniting petrol vapours inside a tanker after it had finished refilling an underground petrol tank at the station.

The *Bangkok Post* printed an article about an incident of this type taking place in Indonesia, which the *China Post* reportedly covered originally. It is speculated that these articles were prompted by the chain e-mails, and not the other way around.

Name:	Ghostly Handprints
Code:	TR8702
Origin:	Early 1970s, USA
Status:	False

UNCOVERED

The Legend

A few years back in a small town in America, a tragic accident happened. A school bus packed with children stalled while travelling over a railway crossing, and a train was heading towards them at great speed. There was no time to evacuate the bus, and the train was travelling so fast it couldn't stop in time. Every child on the bus perished in that fatal accident.

Locally, rumours abounded that the railway crossing was haunted, and a couple of teenagers thought that they would check this rumour out for themselves. They drove to the railway crossing and parked up right over the tracks. After a few minutes, the strangest of things happened: the car started to roll forwards of its own accord. The car continued to roll until it was completely clear of the tracks.

The teenagers jumped out of the car and rushed around to the back of it to see who was pushing it. Nobody was there, but they saw something that made them shudder to the bone. The car was extremely dirty and dusty from the drive out there, and all across the back of the car they could see little handprints in the dust, so small they could only have been made by children.

The Investigation

The Ghostly Handprints has all the hallmarks of a classic ghost legend such as The Vanishing Hitch-hiker (HR4704), but is thought to have originated as late as the early 1970s. The legend is told in a subtle manner, and it is left to your own imagination to fill in the gaps. We are led to believe that the spirits of the deceased schoolchildren pushed the teenagers' car off the tracks and out of harm's way, desperately trying to avoid another tragedy.

There are variants of this legend, but the handprints are a distinct feature in all of them. In one version it is set in the early morning, and the handprints appear in the dew. In another version, the handprints are only seen when the back of the car is inspected using a forensic technique with white powder.

And Finally...

Ghostly Handprints is similar in many ways to the legend of Gravity Hill, in Scotland County (USA). If you stop your car at a certain place on the hill and slip the gear in neutral, your car will start rolling uphill. The legend has it that the spirit of a woman who had crashed and died along that section of the road is trying to push the car uphill to safety. In reality, there is a much more logical and scientific explanation of this strange occurrence, and the supernatural has nothing to do with it. It is simply an optical illusion, nature playing tricks with our eyes. The vehicles at this particular point actually roll downhill; the slight decline looks uphill because of the surrounding landscape. The trees by the side of the road slant slightly down the hill and do not grow completely vertical; this confuses the senses and creates the illusion of moving uphill.

Name:	The Chicken Gun
Code:	TR8703
Origin:	Unknown
Status:	False

UNCOVERED

The Legend

Every year, birds cause millions of pounds' worth of damage to aircraft the world over. To combat the problem of birds damaging an aircraft's windshield, the US FAA (Federal Aviation Administration) have created a device to test the strength of a windshield, and it is known as the 'Chicken Gun'. The Chicken Gun simply fires a chicken (already dead) into the windshield of the aircraft at the same speed at which an aircraft would be travelling. If the windshield doesn't crack with the impact, it is safe to say that it would withstand a real collision in flight.

When British Rail was working on creating a new high-speed train, they asked the FAA if they could use the Chicken Gun to test the impact resistance of the windscreen on the proposed train. The first test was disastrous as the chicken went straight through the windscreen, through the driver's seat, and made a huge indentation in the back wall. The BR engineers started from scratch and repeated the whole test, making sure that every instruction was carried out, but again the same thing happened. A third test was carried out, but again with the same results. Finally, the BR engineers gave up and resigned themselves to asking for help from the FAA. They told the FAA engineer exactly how they carried out the tests, and the calamitous results in detail. The reply was simple: 'Next time, thaw the chicken first!'

The Investigation

The Chicken Gun does actually exist, and it is used to simulate flying birds to test the strength of different parts of an aircraft. The FAA first used a Chicken Gun in 1972 and the UDRI (University of Dayton Research Institute) from 1977. The UDRI reportedly fired dead chickens at speeds of up to 900 mph, using a compressed gas gun with a 30-ft-long barrel. As time went on, the chicken was substituted with a gelatine replacement that had the same mass and density as a chicken. Results are recorded and data is compiled using specialised cameras and lasers.

Now, this is the part where the truth gets a little hazy! The origins of this UL are unknown, but it dates back to at least 1986. In the early versions, the frozen chicken was not fired by bungling british train engineers but by American jet engineers instead. As it stands, there has been no proof that the legend originated from an actual incident, and the origins of the legend are unknown. What is clearly apparent, though, is a condescending tone of superiority over inferior foreigners. What I find interesting is that as time goes on the legend gets more Americanised, and the bungling engineers are no longer American, but, as in the version above, have switched to being British, or any other European nationality.

And Finally...

The threat of flying birds to aircraft is very serious: London Heathrow, for instance, has a continual problem of aircraft damage caused by Canada geese. The damage occurs during landing or take-off, when flocks of migrating geese fly into the flight paths of aircraft.

On average, birds are considered responsible for the deaths of two aircrew members every three to five years, and reportedly cost the US Air Force between $50 and $80 million each year.

Name:	The Road Hog
Code:	TR8704
Origin:	At Least Since 1970, England
Status:	False

UNCOVERED

The Legend

An old gent was taking his time driving along the narrow lanes that led into Bodmin, Cornwall, navigating the sharp turns with care and enjoying the scenery. Suddenly, a sports car came hurtling around the corner, almost forcing the old man's Jaguar off the road and into a bush. As he swerved to avoid a collision, the young woman driving the sports car shouted, 'PIG!' The old man, who was now fuming, leant out of his window and shouted back at the woman, 'You stupid cow!' Still incensed, the old man carried on with his journey, and drove around the corner into a huge pig that was standing in the middle of the road.

The Investigation

The Road Hog is believed to have originated from England, and with the labyrinth-style network of narrow and winding country lanes that sprawl across much of the countryside, the story is easy to believe. In Cornwall especially, the roads look like they have been designed by the local drunk, with high hedges lining both sides of the randomly routed roads, contributing to a high risk of a hazard around every corner.

This humorous UL is short and sharp, but as usual hides a sting in its tail. The old man is very quick to take offence and retaliate verbally to a comment that was intended as a warning of a hazard around the next corner – a hazard that the woman herself has just had to swerve to avoid. Perhaps the moral of this UL is that we shouldn't be too quick to judge, as some things may not be as they first appear.

And Finally...

Although first seen in print in England in 1970, the legend spread across the Atlantic and became Americanised in the 1980s. The American versions were usually based in Oklahoma, and the warning came from a farmer by the side of the road. Another variation similar to the English tale above has a woman shouting the warning, and the man replying, 'You're not so great-looking yourself!'

Name:	Battle of the Ages
Code:	TR8705
Origin:	Unknown
Status:	False

UNCOVERED

The Legend

An old lady out doing her Christmas shopping had trouble parking her car as the car park was packed and every space was taken. After circling around at least a dozen times, she spotted a man loading up his shopping into the back of his car. The lady drove over and parked near the space, waiting patiently for the man to finish loading his car. After what seemed like an eternity, the man climbed into the car and pulled out of the parking space. Before the lady even managed to put her Mercedes into first gear, a 'boy racer' type in his Ford Escort nipped into the space and started to walk away.

'Excuse me!' shouted the lady out of her window. 'I've been waiting for that parking space!'

Without even looking back at her, the 'boy racer' responded, 'Sorry, lady, that's how it is when you're young and quick!'

Extremely annoyed, the lady slipped the Mercedes into first gear and rammed the Escort from behind, denting the rear bumper.

In total disbelief, the boy racer shouted back, 'You can't do that!'

The lady in the Mercedes said, 'That's how it is when you're old and rich!'

156

The Investigation

With road rage being a fashionable topic throughout the media, this story fits in with the current trend of low tolerance and violence on the roads. But road rage is nothing new, and this UL was reportedly heard as far back as the 1960s and 1970s.

The origins of this UL have not been traced, but the story has been told across Europe and the USA. As with most ULs it is usually localised, and falls into the by now familiar 'friend of a friend' category. The make of cars involved vary depending on the country and community where the legend is based. In Britain, we stereotype the Ford Escort as a 'boy racer' car, where in America the equivalent is often a flashy Corvette. The lady always has an upmarket car, usually a Mercedes. The variations that involve the perpetrator's car being an old beaten-up banger highlight how the lady chooses to smash her expensive car into the old banger just to prove a point.

The very appeal of this UL is the fact that the arrogant young man gets his just desserts, and the old lady's fury is something we can all relate to. That smash up the bumper is for every idiot who cuts you up in traffic, every jerk who jumps the queue in front of you when you have been waiting in line for ages, and for every German who creeps down in the middle of the night and puts his or her towel on the sun bed.

And Finally...

A variation of this UL featured in a scene in the 1991 film *Fried Green Tomatoes at the Whistle Stop Café*, an adaptation of the novel of the same name by Fannie Flag.

A similar real-life incident was captured by a CCTV camera in a multi-storey car park and shown on national television. A girl was waiting patiently for a car to pull out of a space, where she obviously wanted to park. But as soon as the other car had pulled out, a young man driving the wrong way through the car park nipped into the space, quickly got out of his car and walked off, ignoring protests from the girl. The footage then shows the girl returning to his car a while later and letting all the air out of his tyres.

Name:	Mr Gay
Code:	TR8706
Origin:	Unknown
Status:	False

UNCOVERED

The Legend

An airline engineer named Mr Gay boarded an aircraft using his company pass. Finding that his designated seat was occupied and not wanting to cause a fuss, Mr Gay sat down in an unoccupied seat nearby. Just before they were due to take-off, another flight was cancelled, and the flight attendants were told that all non-paying passengers would have to disembark to make room for ticketed customers from the cancelled flight.

A flight attendant approached the man sitting in Mr Gay's designated seat and asked, 'Excuse me sir, are you Gay?'

The man, looking very surprised, answered, 'Well, yes I am.'

The flight attendant then responded, 'I'm sorry, sir, you will not be able to take this flight. Please collect your belongings and depart the aircraft.'

The real Mr Gay overheard the conversation and quickly interrupted; 'I'm Gay.' The flight attendant then instructed Mr Gay that he would have to leave the aircraft.

Another man, observing the whole situation, suddenly stood up and defiantly announced, 'I'm gay too. Heck, you can't throw us all off!'

The Investigation

I found myself hitting a brick wall at every turn trying to research the origins of Mr Gay, so I sought assistance from the respected 'Godfather' of UL research, Prof. Jan H. Brunvand, whose approach to UL investigating and insightful books have pushed ULs firmly into popular culture. Replying to the e-mail I sent him, he informed me that he cannot remember where he heard it first, but believes that it may have originated in Australia if not in the USA. Brunvand went on to say that he believes that this story is more of a joke than a legend, and would be told as a joke, with some attempt at so-called 'gay speech patterns' by many people.

I am also of the opinion that this is more of a joke than a legend, and the effective play-on-words formula of this story would not look out of place on a TV comedy sketch show.

And Finally...

A similar version of this legend can be found in Prof. Jan H. Brunvand's book, *Too Good to be True*.

If any of you readers have any further information on the background of this UL, be sure to let me know.

Name:	The Locked-out Pilot
Code:	TR8707
Origin:	1978, USA
Status:	False

UNCOVERED

The Legend

During a flight of a certain unnamed airline, the pilot ordered the co-pilot to take control of the aircraft while he spoke to some of the passengers in First Class. Everything was running smoothly, until the co-pilot desperately needed to use the toilet. He waited and waited for the captain to return, until he got so desperate, he just had to relieve himself. Checking that the altitude was correct, and the sky was clear of traffic, he stuck the aircraft on autopilot and slipped out of the cockpit area and into the crew lavatory.

After relieving himself, the co-pilot went to open the door of the cockpit, only to find it locked. He fiddled around in his pockets trying to find the keys, before realising he had left them in his jacket pocket, hanging up in the cockpit area.

Not wanting to cause a fuss, the co-pilot calmly walked down the aisle and found the captain, who was talking to one of the passengers. He asked the pilot if he could borrow his keys, and the man replied that they were in his jacket. The captain immediately realised that they were both locked out of the cockpit and sprang into action.

Both men ran back up the aisle and the captain reached for the fire axe, then he chopped the door down in front of horrified passengers. After the aircraft was brought back under control again, the embarrassed captain explained to everybody what had happened over the speaker system.

The Investigation

Oral variations of this UL date back to at least 1978, and printed versions appeared in the mid 1980s. There have been many variations of The Locked-out Pilot over the years, but probably none quite so controversial as the version printed in the *Chicago Tribune* travel section (Sunday 6 June 1999) where the story was told as an actual event by the reporter Gabby Plattner. A Zimbabwean airline did not take kindly to being named in the article as the airline involved, as they thought it was damaging to their reputation and could affect Zimbabwe's tourist trade. The author of the article quickly apologised and admitted that the story was not from her own experience, but one that she had heard of instead.

The number of flaws in this legend means that it cannot possibly be true. First of all, the cockpit area would never be left completely unattended at any time during a flight, and even if it was, the cockpit door would not be self-locking, and so cannot be locked shut by accident. Even if the door did get locked accidentally, at least one spare key would be kept in a safe location somewhere else on board. The other obvious major flaw is that a fire axe would never be kept in a position where it could be used as a dangerous weapon, and is more likely to be kept in the cockpit itself.

Of course, all versions of this UL were pre-9/11, and since then cockpit security has been radically revised.

And Finally...

The origins of The Locked-out Pilot are slightly murky and cannot be traced back to any particular incident. The first oral versions were usually told by members of the airline industry to each other, and with this in mind, I believe that the legend originally started out as an in-house joke within the industry.

Name:	The Death Car
Code:	TR8708
Origin:	Europe
Status:	False

UNCOVERED

The Legend: Version 1

The owner of a vintage Bentley was brutally murdered in a gangland killing while sitting in the front of the car. His widow wanted to sell the car, but the blood stains on the seat covers kept reappearing. She tried everything from hand-washing the covers to replacing them completely; the stains were seemingly removed at first, but reappeared after a short period of time.

The widow was desperate to sell the car and brought the asking price down to a ridiculously low price after previous would-be buyers were put off by the reappearing stains. Eventually a gentleman, who wished to remain anonymous, bought the classic Bentley for a meagre £1,000.

The Legend: Version 2

The owner of a red Corvette had driven out into the Nevada desert, parked up, and shot himself in the head. The body was left undiscovered in the car for a whole week, in temperatures well exceeding 100 degrees Fahrenheit. After the police had discovered the body, the car was towed to the nearest garage.

As you can imagine, the heat of the desert had practically putrefied the dead body, and the stench from the car was immense. The whole of the interior was revamped and the Corvette was completely re-painted, but still the smell was unbearable. It was almost as if the stench had seeped into the metal framework, and no matter what they did, they couldn't get rid of it.

The going rate for a Corvette of this class is about $6,000, but because of the stench, the dealer was forced to put the car on the market for only $500. To this day, the red Corvette has not been sold, the smell proving to be unbearable for any potential buyers.

The Investigation

Version 1 is a typically English version of The Death Car, and variations of the legend have been told up and down the country since at least the early 1950s. The English versions always involve a stain and not a bad smell.

Version 2 is typically American, where variations have been traced back to 1938. In the American versions, the car cannot be sold no matter how low the price is brought down; the stench is just too much to bear.

The legend's prototype seems to have originated from Europe, and its roots stem from a lot further back than 1938. As in Version 1, the problem is the blood stains left by the murdered victim.

The make of the car varies depending on the location and period the story is set in, but the chosen make and model is always a classic. Classic cars that have been used in this legend include a Cadillac, Jaguar, Bentley, Rolls-Royce, MG, Ford Model A, Corvette and Buick.

And Finally...

A rare 1959 Eldorado Seville Cadillac only has 2,232 miles on the clock, and was last driven on 8 February 1959. On the night of that particular date, the flamboyant owner of the car, Maurice Gagnon, was kidnapped and shot to death in the car. The car has not been driven since, and still has the original battery, exhaust and tyres. After the Cadillac was impounded by the police as evidence, it was sold to a private collector, John Pfanstiehl, and is now kept at the Car Palace Museum in Massachusetts. Mr Pfanstiehl was aware of the Death Car legend, and had serious doubts as to the authenticity of the Cadillac before he saw it. Although this real-life incident shares many similarities with the Death Car legend, one vital element is missing; the car does not stink and does not have any blood stains.

The US sitcom *Seinfeld* featured this legend in a classic episode called *Smelly Car* in 1993, where a valet's BO problem left a permanent smell in Jerry's car, leaving it unusable.

Name:	The Bedbug Letter
Code:	TR8709
Origin:	1940s or earlier
Status:	Undecided

UNCOVERED

The Legend

A lady on a business trip was making the long journey by train, and had retired for the night in a Pullman's sleeper. Halfway through the night she suddenly awoke feeling very itchy and uncomfortable, and on turning on the light she discovered that her bed was crawling with bedbugs. The lady immediately complained to the porter and asked to be given a new bunk to sleep in, only to be told that there were no vacant bunks left on the train.

After returning from her business trip, she wrote a furious letter to the railway company complaining of her ordeal. A prompt reply came back from the head office assuring the lady that hygiene has always been a top priority of the company, and that they were deeply sorry for her experience. They went on to explain that the porter in her Pullman carriage had been disciplined, and that the whole carriage had now been fumigated. The letter ended by offering the lady a free railway ticket to a destination of her choice as compensation.

The letter was eloquently written and most sincere in its apology – it was even signed by the chairman of the railway himself. There was just one problem; attached to the top of the letter with a paper clip was an office memo note. Obviously meant for internal use only, it read: 'Send this whinging old cow the bedbug letter.'

The Investigation

The Bedbug Letter was first reported in the 1940s, but may go back even further than that. It is unclear whether a true event triggered this legend, as the origins are completely unknown. A letter sent to the editor of *Princeton Alumni Weekly* dated 5 February 1992 claimed the legend dates back to 1889 and that it involves Mr G. Pullman (president of the Pullman Palace Car Company). There is no proof to back up the letter, and it is believed that the letter was written with the tongue placed firmly in cheek.

Modern variations of the Bedbug Letter legend have moved to the skies, with the form of transport being an aircraft. The complaint is normally about cockroaches, and the 'fob-off' letter usually purportedly comes from the airline's public relations manager, with a Post-it note attached reading: 'Send this jerk the Cockroach letter.'

This legend questions the sincerity of apology letters (known in the trade as 'duck letters'), and highlights the real attitude of the company involved. In this case, a slick piece of PR work is completely undone by a memo that was supposed to be for internal viewing only.

In old-time railroad slang, the term 'bedbug' means a Pullman's porter (a piece of trivia for you!).

And Finally...

A real incident similar to this legend happened in November 2000, when Mr Ian Payne, a nurse from Aylesbury, wrote to the

BBC requesting a season of Jean Simmons films, and asked for the autograph of Lorraine Heggessey. The Beeb wrote back to Mr Payne informing him that they could not consider a 'Simmons Season' at this time. Attached to the top of the letter was a Post-it note reading: 'NUTTER, polite fob-off, no autograph.'

A spokesman for the BBC said: 'We have apologised unreservedly to Mr Payne. We have tried to find out who wrote the Post-it note and we have compared the handwriting from the officers and we cannot find anybody's handwriting that matches it. We are mystified at this.'

Name:	Life is Cheap
Code:	TR8710
Origin:	Unknown
Status:	Undecided

UNCOVERED

The Legend

A friend of mine went to stay with relatives who were living in Nigeria. When reading the local newspaper he came across the heading 'MAN FLATTENED IN ROAD ACCIDENT'. He thought that the wording was odd, and wondered why they didn't use a more traditional heading such as 'MAN HIT IN ROAD ACCIDENT'.

After reading the news story, my friend understood the nature of the heading in sickening clarity; a car had knocked down a man and no one had stopped to help. Instead, the passing cars just treated him like road kill, driving over him until he was completely flattened into the ground.

After reading the article, my friend asked one of his relatives why people had not stopped to help or call an ambulance. Their reply was simply: 'Out here, life is cheap.'

The Investigation

My dad told me this story a few years ago and said that one of his friends had told him the story, claiming it had actually involved a friend of his. When we approached my dad's friend recently, he couldn't recall telling the story and said it must have been someone else. Anyone who has ever attempted to trace the origins of a legend will recognise this pattern: it is the old FOAF formula.

This is a great story that capitalises on the recent bad press that certain African countries can be dangerous places for tourists to visit. Although safari holidays are becoming ever more popular, some parts of Africa have been turned into no-go zones because of the high level of violent crime. This helps feed the notion that in certain African areas life is cheap.

And Finally...

I do not know enough about this story to claim that I have uncovered a 'new kid on the block' UL, so it may be safer to label it a proto-legend.

Name:	The JATO Rocket Car
Code:	TR8711
Origin:	Early 1960s, USA
Status:	False

UNCOVERED

The Legend

Police in Arizona were completely baffled after coming across the smouldering remains of a car embedded into the side of a cliff 150 feet high. The damage to the car was so severe that the make and model could not be identified at the scene, nor the explanation of how it got there.

After an intensive forensic and police investigation, the events that led up to the crash were gradually pieced together. A former member of the US Air Force was trying to beat the land speed record and had somehow got his hands on a JATO (Jet Assisted Take-Off) unit. JATO units are normally used on heavy military transport aircrafts to assist with their take-off, and are solid fuel rockets. This man found a long straight stretch of road on the dried lake beds of Arizona, attached a JATO unit onto his 1967 Chevy Impala, then accelerated at high speed before switching on the JATO unit. The Chevy almost immediately reached a speed of around 300 mph, and the driver would have experienced G-forces normally handled by fighter pilots. After a couple of miles the driver would have been unconscious as the Chevy became airborne, the vehicle gradually climbing before impacting with the cliff face 3.9 miles from where the JATO unit was first ignited.

The wreckage of the Chevy was so severe that the driver could only be identified by dental records, and his fingernails were found imbedded in what remained of the steering wheel.

The Investigation

This UL has reached cult status after becoming the Darwin Awards Winner of 1995, and has since become the most popular winner of the Darwin Awards of all time. A brief explanation: the Darwin Awards is an annual honour given to the person who did the gene pool the biggest service by killing themselves in the most extraordinarily stupid way. Although this legend originally fooled the judges of the Darwin Awards, they have since recognised it as being a bogus story.

While this legend has been given a new lease of life since this accolade, the origins go back a lot further than 1995. Original versions have reportedly been heard as far back as the early 1960s, where the car was a 1940s Ford, and the JATO was ignited to escape from pursuing cop cars along a highway, with the car ending up somewhere in the San Francisco Bay.

The legend was more widely spread in the 1970s, proving popular among US military servicemen. These early versions explained how the JATO unit got into the wrong hands in the first place, with it usually being taken from a cargo aircraft or air force base. This little background detail of how the JATO unit was obtained is noticeably missing in the latter-day versions.

In the early 1990s, this gem of a legend reached the vast arena of the World Wide Web, quickly establishing itself in cyberspace through the medium of e-mail. These versions were based in New Mexico, with a Plymouth Road Runner being the make and model of the car involved. In 1995, the car was transformed into a 1967 Chevy Impala, and the location was switched to Arizona. The explosion of popularity that followed firmly established this legend in netlore history.

And Finally...

Is it just me, or does this UL remind you of that classic cartoon *Road Runner*? You know, the one where the coyote goes to extreme measures to try and catch the chirpy Road Runner, but always ends up in spectacular failure. In some episodes, the coyote would strap a large red rocket onto his back while wearing roller skates, and when the Road Runner zoomed past with his chirpy 'Beep, Beep', the coyote would light the rocket hoping to catch up with his target. This usually ended with the coyote plummeting down to earth from the canyon, or colliding head first with a cliff face. Sound familiar? Anyone?

Name:	The Clever Motorist
Code:	TR8712
Origin:	1991, USA
Status:	Undecided

UNCOVERED

The Legend

A man caught speeding on a motorway by a speed camera was sent his penalty fine of £40. He was also sent a photograph of the speeding car, the time and the date, and was informed that three points would be docked from his driving licence.

Decididing to play a little practical joke, the motorist sent back a photo of a cheque payable to the amount of £40. The police then sent him a photo of a pair of handcuffs. The motorist got the message and paid up.

The Investigation

This British version of The Clever Motorist appeared on the scene in 1997, but the story may have originated from a San Francisco newspaper columnist in 1991. Herb Caen told the story about Steve Barkley of Pebble Beach sending the police a photo of $45 in cash, when fined the same amount after being caught speeding by a radar speed trap. A week later, the same columnist followed up the story, and reported that the police had played Steve at his own game by sending him a photo of a pair of handcuffs. Caen finished the column by writing, 'Your move, Steve.'

So, it seems that the legend could have emerged from a real-life incident, although I am not completely convinced of the authenticity of the Steve Barkley story; it seems to be too neatly constructed for my liking. Would the police have the time and patience to play this little game with Mr Barkley? Or, more likely, wouldn't they consider Steve Barkley's prank a waste of police time and not be particularly amused by it?

The British versions tend not to vary a great deal from the American ones, although the photo sent to the police is normally of a cheque, not cash, as in the American versions. The legend is usually localised by the teller, and told as a recent event that has happened.

And Finally...

In Britain, motorists caught speeding by speed cameras have to request that photographic evidence be sent to them if they want proof, at a cost of about £6 (at time of print). Photographic evidence is not sent automatically, as claimed in the British versions of the legend.

Name:	The Wooden Airfield
Code:	TR8714
Origin:	World War Two
Status:	Undecided

UNCOVERED

The Legend

During World War Two, the Germans built a decoy airfield in occupied Holland that was entirely made of wood. The 'airfield' was constructed with such detail that even the hangars, gun emplacements, oil tanks and aircraft were built entirely out of wood. This all took time, and their activity was reported to the allies, who had time to observe and send in photo experts.

Finally, the last wooden plank was laid, and the decoy was finished. Any German celebrations were short-lived, though, as early the next morning, a lone RAF bomber crossed the Channel, flew in low, circled the field once, and dropped a large wooden bomb.

The Investigation

This version of the popular wartime legend has been adapted from the book *Masquerade: The Amazing Camouflage Deceptions of World War II*, written by Seymour Reit (Signet, 1980). The legend was a popular tale amongst the allied forces, especially the RAF, and has been told ever since.

The truth behind the legend may be deeply entwined in wartime propaganda, and part of the psychological war that was being fought out between Churchill and Hitler. Stories like this were often used to boost the morale of the troops, and were deliberately spread amongst the forces during the war for this effect. If the legend were true, the mission carried out by the allied bomber would have been a risky propaganda stunt, carried out to demoralise the Germans and rejuvenate our own troops' flagging spirits. The stunt would have been carried out as a symbol of defiance, and a message to the Germans that the British cannot be outwitted.

The authenticity of the legend is in doubt because it is unlikely that the Germans would have spent so much time building a complex decoy airfield. The bird's-eye view from an aircraft would have been very limited, so only a simple structure would have been needed to achieve the deception. Another question is whether the allies would have risked an expensive aircraft and the life of a much-needed pilot just for a propaganda stunt? Risky missions were carried out for propaganda reasons, but it makes strategic sense to stay one step ahead of the enemy. The allies would have more likely played their cards close to their chest, not giving away what they knew until the time was right.

And Finally...

Decoy airfields were used by both the British and the Germans, playing a vital role in the history of World War Two. To thwart the extensive damage caused by the Luftwaffe (German air force), the British built a complex array of decoy targets, including airfields, placing them miles away from potential key targets. The aim was to fool the Germans into reporting back, and bombing, the decoy targets. With resources running low, the decoys also concealed the vulnerability of the deflated RAF at the time. The British drafted in a whole array of skilled workmen to help construct the decoys, making them look as realistic as possible.

The decoy tactics of the British proved to be successful as the decoy targets were bombed more than the real airfields, wasting thousands of tonnes of German bombs.

CATEGORY:
FOOD AND DRINK

Today we live in a world of fast living and fast food. The rise in popularity of organic food represents a realisation that having our food sprayed, processed, pre-packed, ready made and microwaved may be quick but it is not necessarily a healthy way to eat. Our mistrust of fast-food outlets and cheap supermarket food stems from the worry that the food may not be of the quality we are told it is, and this is reflected in ULs.

This category contains the Kentucky Fried Rat legend (FD3301), probably the most famous UL of all time. Another breakthrough legend for my project is Carrot Vision (FD3308), which provides a good insight into how governments have realised the potential of ULs and have used them to maximum effect with wartime propaganda campaigns. On a personal note, I found American Soup (FD3302) both funny and interesting as my Kosovan friend explained to me how this legend was portrayed back in his homeland. It is a humorous look at the misunderstandings that can occur between two totally different societies. It has a similar tone to the story of when Polish immigrants first moved to America and they thought that dog food tins actually contained dog meat. This is because where they came from all tins had a picture on the front showing what they actually contained. It makes me wonder what they thought was in baby food.

Name:	Kentucky Fried Rat
Code:	FD3301
Origin:	Early 1970s, USA
Status:	False

UNCOVERED

The Legend: Version 1

A woman decided to treat her family to a take-away, and drove down to the local Kentucky Fried Chicken. On the way home, the smell of the chicken was too enticing, and she pulled a piece out of the bucket to eat. She bit into the unusual-shaped piece of chicken, and immediately thought it tasted a bit odd. The woman pulled over to the side of the road, and switched the internal car light on to inspect the piece of chicken. After pulling away a piece of the batter she saw some dark fur and realised with full horror that it was a dead rat. She had just bitten into a Kentucky Fried Rat!

The Legend: Version 2

My friend's father bought a bucket of Kentucky Fried Chicken pieces before entering a cinema. When he had settled into his seat and the lights had dimmed, he decided to tuck into the bucket. He took a bite out of an odd-shaped piece of chicken, and immediately felt some kind of strange ooze run out of his mouth and down his chin.

My friend's father spat out the mouthful of chicken and ran to the toilets to investigate, and was horrified when he saw blood running down his chin. He looked at the piece of chicken and saw what looked like a tail protruding from the crispy coating. On further investigation, he came to the sickening realisation that he had actually bitten into a batter-covered rat.

The Legend: Version 3

Two young couples stopped one night for take-away chicken at a well-known fast-food outlet, and took their food back to the car. While sitting in the car eating their chicken, one of the girls complained that the chicken tasted weird. The driver switched on the light, and the girl discovered that she had been eating a dead battered rodent. The girl went into shock, and was immediately taken to the local hospital.

Apparently, the husband of the sick girl was approached by lawyers representing the fast-food restaurant, and offered a tidy sum of $45,000. After several days, the girl was put on the critical list, the offer went up to $85,000, and this was refused. Unfortunately the girl died, and the fast-food restaurant now has a huge lawsuit on their hands.

The Investigation

The Kentucky Fried Rat was first documented in the early 1970s, and since then it has become one of the most notorious and well-loved ULs of all time. Version 1 was heard in 1974, and is typical of the early US versions. Although the legend has proved to be versatile and there are many variations of the story, certain motifs remain the same. The fast-food outlet is normally KFC, the battered creature is usually a rat, and the unlucky victim is usually a woman.

Version 2 was actually told to me by my good friend David Adams, sometime around the summer of 1990. As detailed in the Introduction, David now believes this happened to a work colleague of his father's. In my friend's belief lies the key to the legend's success and popularity.

Details can differ in each variation, such as a mouse replacing the rat, and the name of the fast-food chain or restaurant involved. However, most variations target large corporate fast-food franchises, and not locally run businesses. As in many ULs, the large corporate businesses are seen as a faceless establishment, and a certain mistrust is shown towards the hygiene of fast 'assembly line' food.

Version 3 is an early example of the legend, taken from a documented version reportedly heard in 1971. This early version includes another important aspect to the legend; lawsuits. There have been many lawsuits over the years involving popular fast-food restaurants, but these have always involved parts of animals being found in food (such as when a battered chicken head was found in a box of McDonald's chicken wings by Katherine Ortega in Virginia, USA). To my knowledge, not one case has involved a whole rat being found.

The Kentucky Fried Rat legend takes a backhanded swipe at the pace of modern society. We are more concerned with how quickly we can get and eat our food than with the preparation of a nutritious and wholesome family meal. Fast food is used as a symbol of contemporary values.

And Finally...

The term 'Kentucky Fried Rat story' is coined in the hit novel *The Beach* by Alex Garland. The main character uses the phrase to label the existence of a secret beach as a UL.

Name:	American Soup
Code:	FD3302
Origin:	Europe
Status:	False

UNCOVERED

The Legend

A man in Kosovo was regularly sent food packages from his relatives who had moved to America. One day, the postal service in his village telephoned the man to inform him that they had another package from America for him to collect. The man's car wouldn't start, so he had to ask his neighbour for a lift. The neighbour reluctantly gave him a lift into the village. The village was within walking distance, but the man was afraid that the package would be too heavy to carry home.

When he collected the package he almost died of embarrassment, as the parcel was no bigger than a can of beans. The neighbour cursed him for wasting his time and they went home.

Inside the package was a small tin of a greyish-black powdery substance. With delight, the man thought that his relatives had sent him some more of that delicious American soup that you only have to pour hot water onto. 'Those clever Americans,' the man said to himself. 'They can turn soup into powder, and then the powder back into soup again.' He wasted no time in making his soup, and although it didn't taste quite as nice as the other

184

ones he had been sent before, he slurped it up with the same enthusiasm. Only after he had finished the last mouthful did the man spot a small note that was included with the package.

After reading the note, the man ran to the toilet and was violently sick. The note had informed him that his Aunt Mary had died, and that the package contained her ashes, which they had sent back for burial in her homeland.

The Investigation

During a conversation about this legend, a good friend of mine from Kosovo told me this version. He remembers hearing this story many times in his homeland, especially after the fall of the Communist State. He also informed me that the story was always told with a humorous tone, and was never taken seriously. Stand-up comedians recited the story as part of their act, a tongue-in-cheek jibe at their own countrymen's bedazzlement by Western technology and culture.

The Kosovan version circulated after the country was freed from the shackles of Communism, and introduced to the Western world. Throughout the 1990s, people from this unstable, war-torn country have struggled bitterly against poverty. Many Kosovans have emigrated or become refugees in other countries. Stories from these relatives about Western society have probably fuelled the legend.

This modern version of the UL, often named 'Accidental Cannibalism', has parallels with the original versions that became widespread in the years shortly after World War Two. In Britain, the war had taken its toll, money was scarce and food rations were in place for many years following. Powdered food was available under the ration restrictions, as well as being included in some relief packages. In other European countries, people had fled their homeland to escape persecution, and shipped back food to their poor relatives.

The true origins of the legend may have a more sinister anti-Semitic tone, from back in the days of the Renaissance. An old story tells of an Italian Jew that smuggled his dead friend's body back to Venice, by chopping the body into manageable pieces and pickling them in large jars with spices and honey. Then he transported the jars by boarding a ship bound for Venice. A Gentile from Florence nicked a couple of pieces from the jars, and unwittingly feasted upon them.

American Soup is a story of misunderstanding between two very different cultures, and the difficulties that arise when a nation tries to adapt too quickly to an unfamiliar modern culture. It is also a story of unintentional cannibalism, the very thought of which not only conjures up powerful feelings of loathing and disgust, but also of thought-provoking curiosity.

And Finally...

In 1906, Upton Sinclair wrote *The Jungle*, which exposed the appalling conditions in Chicago's meat-packing industry. This controversial novel caused an outrage, which climaxed with the Pure Food and Drug Act being passed in the same year. In one of the worst stories, a worker slips and falls into a large vat of meat being rendered for lard. The bones were eventually fished out of the vat, but the body had already been dissolved. This didn't stop production, and that batch of Durham's Pure Leaf Lard was shipped out, bound for kitchen cupboards across America.

Stories like this one shocked the American public, and the US Department of Agriculture was forced to investigate whether the stories were true or not. They were found to be true. Congress even had to call hearings to pacify an angry public, incensed that they had taken part in accidental cannibalism.

Radical changes were made to the law in the meat industry, culminating with America's first ever Meat Protection Act in 1906.

Name:	Bar Peenuts
Code:	FD3303
Origin:	Unknown
Status:	Undecided

UNCOVERED

The Legend: Version 1

My sister and her boyfriend were visiting friends in Sri Lanka, and on one evening they all went to a local bar. Bowls of nuts were provided at the bar as free snacks, and my sister's boyfriend, never one to pass up an opportunity of free food, spent most of his time at the bar nibbling on nuts.

By the time the evening was out, my sister's boyfriend was complaining of stomach cramps, and was violently sick when they got back to their friends' house. He was still very ill the next day, and was baffled as to what could have caused it. It was then that the friends' father told him a disturbing fact about bar nuts. Apparently, a bowl of nuts had been taken away for analysis by health inspectors, and the results were shocking. On one single nut, they found traces of seven different kinds of urine. This is caused by people not washing their hands after they have been to the toilet.

My sister's boyfriend has vowed never to eat bar snacks again.

The Legend: Version 2

Health officials are urging restaurant owners not to hand out unwrapped mints to customers after a meal. The warning follows an investigation that found small traces of urine and fecal coliform bacteria in restaurant mint dishes.

Another study has revealed that 80 per cent of people do not wash their hands after going to the toilet.

The Investigation

There is definitely some truth behind this UL, but how far the truth stretches is debatable. It is a fact that some states in America have ordered restaurants not to supply unwrapped courtesy sweets for their customers, unless it is done in an appropriate manner (e.g. using a dispensing machine). This action has been prompted by advice from health officials that unwrapped sweets could pose a health risk, and not based on any facts taken from an investigation.

Version 1 was actually told to me by my sister's boyfriend, and he really did become quite sick while they were on holiday. Although there is no proof that this was caused by eating the peanuts provided at the bar, he firmly believes that that was the reason. The very thought that the food could contain traces of urine sickens most people, but also seems very plausible. This may be because we know from our own experiences that many people do not wash their hands after going to the toilet.

Version 2 is more like a news bulletin, and is more typical of the American versions. Generally, they are always backed up by research statistics, although the authenticity of the statistics is questionable. In the *Straits Times Interactive*, a reporter named Arti Mulchand wrote an article covering the subject. Arti claims to have done her own research by watching people go in and come out of a pub toilet. Arti claims that over half the people didn't wash their hands, and that included staff.

And Finally...

It is generally recognised that unwrapped sweets pose a health risk from not only unwashed hands but also other elements of our surroundings. Although our American friends have now opted for wrapped sweets, the British have not heeded the warning as many low star hotels and Indian restaurants have unwrapped courtesy mints in bowls.

Remember: always wash your hands!

Name:	Neiman Marcus Cookies
Code:	FD3304
Origin:	At least since 1948
Status:	False

UNCOVERED

The Legend

My daughter and I had just finished a delicious salad at the Neiman Marcus café in Dallas, and decided to have a small dessert. Being such cookie lovers as we are, we decided to try the Neiman Marcus Cookie.

The cookie was excellent, and I asked the waitress if I could have the recipe. With a small frown, she replied, 'I'm afraid not.'

'Well,' I said, 'would you let me buy the recipe?'

With a cute smile, the waitress responded, 'Yes.' After I asked how much, she said, 'Only two fifty – it's a great deal!' Amazed at how cheap the recipe was, I told the waitress to add it to my tab.

At the end of the month I received a Visa statement, and was amazed that I had been billed $285 by Neiman Marcus. I remembered that I had spent almost $10 on the two salads, and had bought a scarf for about $20. As I glanced at the bottom of the statement, it read 'Cookie Recipe – $250.00'.

I immediately called Neiman's customer services department, and informed them that I had been quoted 'two fifty' by the waitress, and under no interpretation does 'two fifty' mean $250! Neiman Marcus refused to budge. They would not refund my money, because according to them what the waitress had told me was not their problem. And because I had seen the recipe, there was no way that they could refund the money.

Angrily, I informed the woman on the other end of the phone that they could have my $250, but I was going to make sure that every cookie lover with an e-mail address would receive the recipe for free.

'I wish you wouldn't do that.' The customer services woman replied.

'Well, you should have thought about that before you decided to rip me off!' I responded.

So here it is!!

Please, please pass this recipe on to everyone you know. I paid $250 for this, and I don't want Neiman Marcus to get another penny for this recipe...

The Investigation

This classic piece of netlore has been in circulation since at least 1989, and is usually found in the form of an e-mail. The example printed above is a typical e-mail version, and is usually followed by the supposed actual recipe for a Neiman Marcus Cookie. The legend has been totally debunked, and up to recently there was no such thing as a Neiman Marcus Cookie. In fact, Neiman Marcus only created a chocolate chip cookie through demand generated by the legend. Now that's what I call negative marketing.

Before setting its sights firmly on Neiman Marcus, the legend briefly targeted a Chicago department store named Marshall Fields. Before that, in the 1980s, the legend was attached to the USA-based Mrs. Fields company, who sell cookies and baked goods. Similar formula, except the misunderstanding about the 'two fifty' took place during a request for the recipe over the telephone to the head office. A verbal misunderstanding on the telephone is maybe more believable than the Neiman Marcus Cookie version, as surely the person would have noticed the amount when they signed the credit card slip to pay the bill.

To find the true origins of the legend we have to look back a lot further than that, though, possibly as far back as the 1930s and '40s. In fact, a similar story has been found in a cookbook dating back to 1948. The book *Massachusetts Cooking Rules, Old and New* explains how a lady had asked a chef on a train for the recipe for the fudge cake that she was eating. The chef gladly sent her the recipe, and billed her $25. Her attorney advised her to pay the amount, so she sent the recipe to all her friends, hoping they would get some pleasure from it.

In the 1950s, the famous Red Velvet Cake legend was born. This time, the spotlight was firmly fixed on the world famous Waldorf-Astoria Hotel in New York City. The legend tells of a woman who had the Red Velvet Cake for dessert, and asked the management for the recipe. The hotel obliged, and sent her the recipe together with a bill for $300. Of course, she got her own back by sending out the recipe to everyone she knew. The legend hung over the hotel like a dark cloud, before moving on and attaching itself to the Mrs. Fields Company in the 1980s. To combat the legend, the Waldorf-Astoria Hotel gives away the recipe for the Red Velvet Cake to anyone who asks for it – for free!

And Finally...

The following recipe for chocolate chip cookies can be found on the Neiman Marcus website. The website informs you that you can copy it, print it out, and pass it along to friends and family – and it's absolutely free.

Neiman Marcus Chocolate Chip Cookie Recipe

Ingredients
½ cup unsalted butter, softened
1 cup brown sugar

3 tablespoons granulated sugar
1 egg
2 teaspoons vanilla extract
½ teaspoon baking soda
½ teaspoon baking powder
½ teaspoon salt
1 ¾ cups flour
1 ½ teaspoons instant espresso powder, slightly crushed
8 ounces semi-sweet chocolate chips

Directions
Cream the butter with the sugars until fluffy.
Beat in the egg and the vanilla extract.
Combine the dry ingredients and beat into the butter mixture.
Stir in the chocolate chips.
Drop by large spoonfuls onto a greased cookie sheet. Bake at 190 degrees Celsius for 8 to 10 minutes, or 10 to 12 minutes for a crispier cookie. Makes 12 to 15 large cookies.

Name:	Don't Swallow your Gum
Code:	FD3305
Origin:	Unknown
Status:	False

UNCOVERED

The Legend

HEALTH WARNING

Do not swallow chewing gum!

The gum is indigestible, which means your body cannot digest it. It will take a staggering seven years for the gum to pass completely through your digestive system.

The Investigation

The above message is a typical warning notice that usually arrives in the form of an e-mail. Parents have been telling their kids not to swallow their gum for this very reason for years, and so the legend is nothing new. Chewing gum is indigestible, and it is that term that has caused so much confusion. The simple fact is that although swallowing your gum is not one of the healthiest of things to do, the gum will pass straight through your system, and into your stool undigested. Although experts argue that swallowing large amounts of sugar free gum could cause diarrhoea, this is because the sugar substitutes are not absorbed and pass into the small intestine and colon. So to sum it up, if you swallow gum, it will not stay in your stomach for seven years. But if you swallow an excessive amount of sugar free gum, it will give you the splats. Is that clear to everyone?

Chewing gum has an interesting history. Ancient Greeks chewed a form of mastic gum as far back as 50 AD. It was made from the resin obtained from the bark of the mastic tree, and was called mastiche. The Greek women used the gum to freshen their breath and to clean their teeth.

The ancient Mayans of Central America also chewed the resin obtained from sapota trees. The name of the resin was chicle, and plays an important role in the history of chewing gum.

During the 1860s, Antonio Lopez de Santa Anna, several times president of Mexico and famed for orchestrating the bloody battle of Alamo, introduced chicle to Thomas Adams, a New Yorker. The idea was to use chicle as a rubber substitute, but history had other plans, as it was found to be more useful as a base for chewing gum.

And Finally...

New research shows that chewing gum could increase your brainpower. In a joint study carried out by the University of Northumbria and the Cognitive Research Centre in Reading, results showed that chewing gum increased thinking power and improved memory.

In experiments, people who had been chewing gum had an increased heartbeat of three beats a minute faster than those who hadn't chewed gum. This is probably because the chewing action improves the delivery of glucose and oxygen to the brain, which would make the person more alert.

Another theory is that chewing gum causes a surge of insulin, due to the mouth watering in anticipation for a meal. There are insulin receptors in the brain, which are important for learning and memory.

Name:	Cokecaine
Code:	FD3306
Origin:	1885
Status:	True

UNCOVERED

The Legend

Cocaine was used in the original recipe of the Coca-Cola drink.

The Investigation

It's hard to believe, but the Class A drug cocaine was used as part of the original Coca-Cola formula. Coca-Cola was given its name in 1885, and was marketed as a tonic for most common ailments, based on the two medicinal main ingredients which consisted of extracts of coca leaves and kola nuts. The exact amount of cocaine that was used in the original recipe is not certain, but only after a few years was the amount dropped considerably. The reason being that by the mid 1890s, the harmful effects of cocaine were being realised and the use of cocaine was starting to be frowned upon. It is reported that Coca-Cola still had to include traces of the drug as an ingredient, to protect the trade name of the drink. In the early days, the syrup had not been patented, so the name with its reference to coca leaves (cocaine) was a very valuable asset.

The exact year that Coca-Cola stopped using cocaine as an ingredient altogether is not certain, as it varies considerably from source to source. It is widely believed that all traces of the drug were removed from the formula in 1905, but another source reports that cocaine was not completely left out until the late 1920s.

And Finally...

This legend is part of a much bigger group of ULs, commonly known as 'cokelore'. The global success of the Coca-Cola Company has been spectacular to say the least, and the number of ULs associated with Coca-Cola is a fair reflection of that success. Probably the only other company that could claim such an extensive volume of legends associated with it is the Walt Disney Company.

Cokelore legends range from true accounts to the ridiculous, and include such classics as Coca-Cola Used to be Green, claims that the Mormons own the company, and that a mouse was once found in a Coke bottle. In case you were wondering, the first two are most definitely false, but the mouse in the bottle may be based on a true event (scary thought!).

Name:	Santa Coke
Code:	FD3307
Origin:	1930s
Status:	False

UNCOVERED

The Legend

Coca-Cola originally created the modern-day image of Santa Claus as an old, tubby but jolly man, dressed in a red and white robe. The image was part of a seasoned Coca-Cola advertising campaign, and has Santa Claus wearing their corporate colours of red and white.

The Investigation

The familiar image of Father Christmas/Santa Claus is known throughout the world, and is probably the most familiar symbol of this festive time of year. But things haven't always been that way, and the history of the big chubby fella is a complex mixture taken from different myths, legends and folklore stories.

The modern-day Santa Claus has been moulded from two separate traditional religious figures. The first is St Nicholas, the elf-like gift-bringer, and the second is Kriss Kringle. The name Kriss Kringle derives from 'Christkindlein', which means 'child of Christ', and this character was part of the Christmas tradition over much of mainland Europe. The American version of Santa Claus originates from the Dutch figure of 'Sinter Klaas', who was introduced to America by Dutch settlers in New Amsterdam (now known as New York). The tradition of Sinter Klaas is based on the myth of St Nicholas, and the Dutch tradition picked up momentum when the New York Historical Society was founded in 1804, with St Nicholas as its patron saint.

In 1823, Clement C. Moore wrote a poem for his children titled 'A Visit From St. Nicholas'. The poem was later published, and included the now legendary picture of Santa Claus by Thomas Nast. The poem and the picture combined are probably one of the most prominent factors in forming the modern-day Santa Claus.

The American image of Santa Claus only became standardised after the British tradition of Christmas cards was introduced to America, which in 1885 featured the familiar red-and-white-suited Father Christmas.

The Coca-Cola Company first used an image of Santa Claus in their advertising during the 1920s, their adverts appearing in magazines far and wide. The image of the Santa they created was similar to the work of the caricaturist Thomas Nast and was rather stern and serious looking.

In 1930, Santa appeared in the seasonal Coca-Cola advertising campaign again, this time the artist Fred Mizen painting a department-store Santa that was used in print ads. The campaign was successful, but Coca-Cola wanted a more realistic and symbolic Santa Claus for the next campaign.

In 1931, Coca-Cola turned to the talented Haddon Sundblom for their latest Christmas advertising campaign. Sundblom wanted a warmer, friendlier and more approachable Santa, and so turned to Clement C. Moore's poem 'A Visit From St. Nicholas' for inspiration. The results were a slightly plump, jolly and elf-like Santa. Haddon Sundblom painted these Santa Claus portraits for the next 35 years.

As far as I am aware, Coca-Cola do not claim that they created the modern image of Santa Claus, merely that they helped create it; which is arguably true. The modern image of Santa may have been moulded from the talents of Clement C. Moore and Thomas Nast, but it was Haddon Sundblom's vision and Coca-Cola's mass commercialism that standardised the image of Santa Claus globally.

And Finally...

Of course, in Britain we have our own Father Christmas, who differs slightly in appearance from Santa Claus, as he has a longer beard and coat. The legend of Father Christmas originates from Finland, where its roots are in an old pagan tradition. The original Joulupukki (Father Christmas) was a frightening creature who didn't give presents, but demanded them instead. Over the years, with the influence of Christian beliefs and local traditions, the Joulupukki was transformed into the lovable Father Christmas we know today.

Name:	Carrot Vision
Code:	FD3308
Origin:	World War Two
Status:	True

UNCOVERED

The Legend

During World War Two, the RAF bragged that the great accuracy of their fighter pilots at night was the result of them being fed enormous quantities of carrots. The Germans bought the story because their folklore wisdom incorporates the same myth that eating carrots helps you to see in the dark. In actual fact, the success of the RAF pilots was due to the highly efficient, newly installed on-board radars. By utilising the old folk tale, the British RAF managed to disguise the use of radar.

The Investigation

So it seems that the line 'Eat up your carrots, it will help you see in the dark', was used by mums in both England and Germany. There were other logical reasons why the Germans bought the story so easily, but I will come to that in a minute. Firstly, let's look at the importance of radar, and the impact it had during the war.

World War Two was unique in many ways, one of them being that it was the first war where intelligence gathering was seen as a weapon over bullets and bombs. The modern day secret services and military special ops (such as SAS and SBS) were really born out of this war. At times, it was almost as if Hitler and Churchill were playing the war like a game of chess, each one trying to guess the other's move and to counter-attack. Before radar, advanced warning of enemy aircraft depended solely on how quickly they were visually spotted. Radar cut the response time, and made it easier for allied pilots to locate and intercept enemy aircraft. When radar systems were fitted onto allied bombers, night raids into enemy territory could be made with a high level of accuracy.

It is not completely certain whether the rumour spread about the carrot-eating pilots was used to disguise the successful interception of enemy night raids, or to disguise the highly accurate allied night-time bombing raids on enemy territory. I believe it was the latter. In 1942, the GEE (standing for Grid) system, a pulse-phasing radar system, was introduced with the receiving equipment fitted on-board aircraft. It was the first radar device to be installed on bombers, and was used as a navigational aid during night raids. The GEE system was a success, and the government were intent on keeping its use top secret and out of enemy hands.

So, to keep the Germans guessing, the British government used the rumour as a smokescreen. Just like in The Wooden Airfield (TR8714), the British government harnessed the potential and power of ULs when used as part of wartime propaganda. But the old myth about carrots was not the only reason why the Germans fell hook, line and sinker. German intelligence also knew that the British had been experimenting with high carotene varieties to try and reduce the effects of night-blindness for pilots. Because of the experiments, the British had a large stock of carrots, and cleverly used this fact to fuel the rumour that the RAF pilots had developed superb night vision due to the consumption of large numbers of carrots.

And Finally...

I suppose you are wondering whether the old myth about eating carrots is true? To answer that question bluntly, no. But carrots contain a reasonable amount of vitamin A. Vitamin A is vital for our body, and lack of it could lead to blindness and defective growth.

CATEGORY:
AROUND THE WORLD

This category is a round-trip cruise exploring ULs from the four corners of the earth. We have The Gucci Kangaroo (AW1901) from down under; an amusing tale with many variations, which has now been made into a feature film titled Kangaroo Jack. We have an absolutely horrific offering from Japan called Honeymoon Horror (AW1903). In Europe we have The Beast Of Belgium (AW1908), a ridiculous tale that mixes the Antichrist with Big Brother (you have to read it to believe it!). Nearer home still, we have the remarkable but true story of a refugee who has been stranded at the Charles de Gaulle Airport in Paris for more than a decade in Home Is Where The Airport Is (AW1910).

This selection of ULs is a mere sprinkling compared to the mass volume in circulation worldwide. I suppose you could say that this is actually more of a whistle-stop tour than a cruise, a tiny glimpse of what this category has to offer. It would be impossible to cover all the legends from around the world, as each country has such a vast and rich supply embroidered into the very fabric of their own societies. To give this category justice, a book of legends from each and every country would need to be produced.

ULs can be a useful tool in understanding the different cultures of a country as they often represent the views, politics, fears and anxieties of the people.

Name:	The Gucci Kangaroo
Code:	AW1901
Origin:	1902, Australia
Status:	False

UNCOVERED

The Legend

During the Americas Cup, held in the waters of Perth, Western Australia, a group of Gucci representatives who were sponsoring the Italian yacht team decided to look for kangaroos to kill time in between races. They had cruised the outback all afternoon trying to spot a 'roo and had just about given up when one jumped out straight in front of their Land Rover. Unable to avoid the unfortunate animal, they skidded into it, knocking him down with a bone-shuddering thud.

Instead of feeling saddened by the dreadful accident, the Italians felt quite pleased with their catch. They propped the motionless kangaroo up against the side of the Land Rover, dressed him in a pair of Gucci sunglasses and one of the representatives' Gucci jacket, and began taking photos.

It was at this point that the animal, which had only been stunned, jumped up and bounded off, still wearing the sunglasses and jacket. The loss of the jacket, though expensive, wouldn't have been so bad… if the Land Rover's keys had not been in the inside pocket.

The Investigation

The earliest found version of this UL dates back to 1902 from Australia, and was traced to a book called *Aboriginalities* by Australian folklorist Bill Scott. In that version a train and not a car knocked out the kangaroo and, of course, he didn't make off with a Gucci jacket to add to his collection. In fact, the kangaroo must have quite an extensive wardrobe judging by all the variations to the legend. Over the years he has not only got away with Gucci jackets, but also Ray-Ban sunglasses, expensive cameras, baseball caps, crew jackets, passports and expensive jewellery to boot. I think the kangaroo is setting himself up for quite a jumble sale out there in the outback.

The Italians are not the only callous foreigners who got their just desserts. 1950s versions were told about the English cricket team, and in more recent years, the Canadian yacht team. All these versions underline a feeling of mistrust towards foreigners, highlighting the lack of respect shown towards the host nation. Just for a cheap prank, the visitors act disgracefully and pay the price. The kangaroo gets the last laugh, and that's fair dinkum', mate!

During the 1960s the UL hit celebrity status, and became associated across America with the 'The Kingston Trio'. The Kingston Trio were a popular folk music group, and one member told the legend as a personal experience that had actually happened to him while the group were touring Australia.

And Finally...

Another American UL exists that is very similar to this one, called The Deer Departed. The story goes that while a man was hunting in a forest, he managed to shoot down a stag with huge antlers. He set up his camera on a tripod and posed with the animal, placing his expensive high-powered rifle with its telescopic sight across the stag's antlers. Only startled, the stag jumped back onto its feet and leapt off into the forest, with the rifle still firmly placed between its antlers!

These 'animals' revenge' stories may have originated from the late 1890s, when the stories were rife in both America and Australia. These tales were normally about a cruel man who tied a stick of dynamite to the tail of an animal (e.g. dog, coyote, rabbit) as an evil prank. The joke always backfired when the animal ran into the man's house.

Name:	Flatjack
Code:	AW1902
Origin:	South Africa
Status:	False

UNCOVERED

The Legend

A young lady was driving her 4x4 Jeep along a stretch of road on the outskirts of Johannesburg that is notorious for carjackings, when she suddenly saw an abandoned car, sideways on, in the middle of the road right in front of her. Realising that this may be a ploy by carjackers to stop her car, she stepped on the accelerator and swerved off the road onto the bumpy grass shoulder, skidding back onto the road after she had passed the abandoned car. On reaching home, the woman phoned the police and told them what she had seen. Thinking that was an end to it, she went to bed.

Early the next morning, the lady was awoken by the police wanting more information on what had actually happened the previous evening. She told them in great detail of how she had taken her 4x4 off the road at speed, passing the abandoned car by driving on the long grass verge and then skidding back onto the road. The police informed the lady that in doing so, she must have run over and killed four men who were lying in wait to ambush her.

The Investigation

Carjacking is a relatively new phenomenon in Britain, with a very small percentage of cases ending in murder. South Africa is different, and has the highest carjacking rate in the world. In a country that has a population of 40 million, there are roughly 16,000 carjackings a year, and 57 of those will end in a person being murdered. The ratio of carjackings to population is 18 times greater than that in the USA. So it's easy to see why carjacking in South Africa is taken as a very serious threat, and, as always, ULs are used to express this fear.

This legend was rampant during the mid 1990s, especially widely known throughout the whole of South Africa. In a country that is gripped by fear of crime, it is not surprising that a legend providing such a sense of poetic justice is so popular. The accidental death of the would-be carjackers can't fail to rouse a triumphant 'what goes around comes around' attitude among the legend's audience.

And Finally...

The fight against carjacking has been cranked up a notch or two by fed-up South Africans, and there are plenty of self-defence courses that teach you the best ways in dealing with such a situation if it happens to you. Advice includes always keeping the car doors locked when travelling, and for women to keep their car rolling, even at traffic lights showing red. Statistics show that the most vulnerable time for motorists are between the times of 4 p.m. and 8 p.m.; just before it gets dark. Tuesdays and Fridays are the days motorists are most likely to encounter a carjacking. The most vulnerable places have proved to be driveways, supermarkets, schools and traffic lights.

Where conventional methods have failed in the fight against carjacking, South Africans are turning to ever more ingenious weapons and gizmos for protection. Such items include a flame-thrower that shoots out of the driver's side door; a shotgun device that is mounted under the driver's seat and can be operated by remote control; and a chassis-mounted spring-loaded sword.

Name:	Honeymoon Horror
Code:	AW1903
Origin:	Japan
Status:	False

UNCOVERED

The Legend

A newly wed couple from Japan went to Thailand for their honeymoon and decided to go shopping for clothes. The young wife spent many hours looking for dresses, and found a few that she liked in a trendy looking fashion store. She went to the dressing room to try them on while her husband waited outside.

After a long while, the husband became anxious as his wife hadn't reappeared from the dressing room, and asked a member of staff to investigate. What they found was that the girl had simply disappeared. After a lengthy police investigation, to no avail, the young Japanese man gave hope of ever seeing his wife again, and went back to Japan a broken man.

Five years passed. The man had just about got over the disappearance of his wife and had managed to piece his life back together when a friend who had been on holiday in the Philippines claimed to have seen his wife. With regret, the friend told the man that he had seen his wife in a sex freak show, with each of her legs and arms horribly mutilated.

It came to light that the dressing room where the wife had disappeared from had a trapdoor to the floor below. A well-organised gang of kidnappers were waiting below, and she had been sold into a prostitution ring.

The Investigation

This incredible tale is widespread across Japan, and certainly seems to feed on fears of abduction. Although tales of abduction are common throughout the world, in Japan they are told with a little more conviction, to the extent that girls warn each other about trapdoors in changing rooms when shopping alone.

The fact that most Japanese versions of this legend happen in a foreign country probably suggests a deep-rooted mistrust of the outside world and an uncertainty of foreign cultures. Yet it must be said that the legend is very similar to other American and European ULs, where girls are kidnapped in clothes shop changing rooms and sold into 'white slavery' as prostitutes.

And Finally...

The chances of this UL actually happening is very unlikely, but the fears behind the legend are completely justified. Human trafficking has become a problem the world over, and the gangs behind it are extremely well organised. These gangs prey on the vulnerable, often targeting girls from poor backgrounds. They are lured abroad by promises of money and jobs, and then sold into prostitution rings. Once abroad, they are trapped. The girls cannot escape, as they have no money, papers or passports, and live under constant fear of their capturers.

Name:	Flying Cows
Code:	AW1904
Origin:	Russia
Status:	False

UNCOVERED

The Legend

A Russian rescue crew plucked some Japanese fishermen from the sea after their vessel had capsized. The Russian authorities quickly detained the fishermen when they claimed that flying cows had sunk their boat.

The story sounded ridiculous, until Russian investigations began unravelling a bizarre set of events that appeared to lead to the vessel being sunk by cows falling from the sky.

Apparently, a couple of Russian air force members had decided to smuggle two cows back home from a Serbian airfield by hiding the animals in the bomb bay of their aircraft. Everything was fine until the aircraft reached and cruised at a colder altitude, and then the cows went berserk.

To save themselves and the aircraft, the crew hastily decided to open the bomb hatch, dropping the cows thousands of feet onto the deck of the unfortunate vessel down below.

The Investigation

Flying cows – I love it! The legend has been around for years, but only reached notoriety when the German Embassy in Moscow

213

reported the story to the German Foreign Ministry in Bonn in the mid 1990s. A German newspaper got hold of the story and printed it.

The fact that the legend burst onto the scene at this particular time may be the influence of a popular 1995 Russian film called *Osobennosti Natsionalnoy Okhoty* (catchy name!) known in English as 'Peculiarities of the National Hunt', which features a similar story.

The film cannot be credited for the legend, though, as this UL had been recorded and printed many times before the film was even made. *The Moscow Times* printed an article on the story on 1 June 1990. The Russians have also told the story as a joke for years.

And Finally...

The legend is very similar to a story heard in Scotland in 1965. A driver explains rather gingerly to police how a flying cow landed on the bonnet of his car, causing him to crash. Unfazed police told him that a lorry driver reported hitting a cow, but couldn't find the body anywhere. The speed and weight of the lorry must have sent the cow flying a considerable distance back down the road, landing on the bonnet of the gentleman's Austin.

Name:	Sounds Like Enemy Whales
Code:	AW1905
Origin:	Unknown
Status:	Undecided

UNCOVERED

The Legend

Swedish naval experts were convinced that foreign submarines were operating in Swedish waters, and the foreign secretary made a strong-worded speech at a UN Conference. Despite this, no foreign government claimed responsibility for using submarines in Swedish waters. The Swedish government decided to launch a massive naval operation to uncover the perpetrators.

After weeks of searching the waters and the painstaking task of tracking sonic sounds under the sea, it was concluded that the perpetrators were not enemy submarines, but a school of whales. Even so, the Vice-Admiral of the Swedish Navy is still convinced that foreign submarines are operating in Swedish waters.

The Investigation

This wonderful legend may or may not be true, but it certainly touches on a sensitive subject of underwater noise pollution including the low frequency sounds emitted from machinery in ships and submarines, and the low frequency sonar sounds sent out to detect enemy submarines. Sonar sounds have been used by ships since World War Two, but advances in technology and the development of near silent submarines has meant that a new active sonar has been developed to bounce off submarines instead of crew having to wait until the submarines are close enough to hear. The problem with this is that the low frequency sonar sounds wreak havoc amongst the marine life. Whales depend on sound as we depend on sight, and they use sonar sound to find food, attract a mate, detect enemies, and to communicate with their young. The man-made sonar sounds can interrupt and drown out these natural sounds, and can even cause deafness, disrupt migration patterns – as could be the case for the school of whales featured in this legend – and at worst cause death amongst the whales.

Another aspect of this legend is that despite the ever-increasing advances in technology, we are still all prone to human mistakes. The idea that the sonar sounds from submarines and those of whales is very similar is given credibility by another fact; after the Cold War had ended, the US Navy handed over its supersensitive hydrophones to a research project called Whales '93. This equipment, now used for monitoring whales, was first used as a means to detect enemy submarines.

The debate concerning the use of high intensity active sonar systems has heated up during the last few years, with the news that the US Navy intend to use such a system to detect and track enemy submarines. According to Navy sound charts, the LFAS (low frequency active sonar) signal can be 140 db when more than 300 miles from its source. It is claimed that this has caused the death of some whales from brain haemorrhage and it could affect all species of marine mammals. It is also claimed that NATO are developing a similar system alongside many countries. This brings fresh concerns over the impact on marine life when all these systems are used simultaneously on a cumulative level.

And Finally...

In another bizarre news story that has supposedly been reported by *The Times*, the Soviets sold 27 marine mammals to Iran. The marine mammals, which include dolphins and beluga whales, had been trained by the Soviet military, and were sold as part of a mass post-Cold War sell-off. The marine mammals had been trained to distinguish between the sounds of friendly and enemy submarine engines, and can even locate missing torpedoes and missiles.

I must admit, this news story smells fishy to me.

Name:	Vote Donald Duck
Code:	AW1906
Origin:	Sweden
Status:	False

UNCOVERED

The Legend

The results of the Swedish general election a few years ago caused much controversy. The Social Democrats, Conservatives and Green Party fared as expected, but some of the other voting results caused uproar amongst politicians in the Riksdag (Swedish parliament).

For some peculiar reason, nearly 13,000 people cast their vote for Donald Duck, which is nearly enough votes to win a seat in the Riksdag. Other strange results included Keith Richards (from rock band The Rolling Stones) with an impressive 14,000 votes, Mick Jagger (also from The Rolling Stones) with 500, Bill Gates with 250, and the Pope with 100 votes. Flagging well behind was the 'Queen of Pop' herself, Madonna, with just 1 vote!

The Investigation

I decided to stay with Sweden a while longer, as this UL really is too good to pass by. Although claimed by many (including reputable websites) to be true, the simple truth is that Donald Duck did not receive 13,000 votes. Sofia Knapp of the Election

Authority in Sweden also informed me that even if he had, it would not have been enough to gain a seat in the Riksdag. Yet, although the details in this story are not correct, there is a political party in Sweden called the 'Donald Duck Party'.

This UL is widely believed because Swedish voters used to have the right to freely erase or add names of their choice on the voting slip. The voting system has since been revised, and the voters no longer have these rights.

I would like to know why Keith Richards is claimed to have got a staggering 13,500 more votes than fellow band member Mick Jagger, and Madonna must be disappointed with her result.

And Finally...

Why Donald Duck? In one source of information, I read that over the Christmas period, the Swedes traditionally watch Donald Duck cartoons on TV. It is as traditional for them as the Queen's speech and eating mince pies are to us.

Perhaps somebody should inform the Swedes that Donald Duck is just a character from a CARTOON, and that he is NOT REAL. Mind you, I can see the appeal of Donald Duck over most politicians.

Name:	The Italian Job
Code:	AW1907
Origin:	Spring 1993, Italy
Status:	Undecided

UNCOVERED

The Legend

An Italian family living in a village near the border with Slovenia decided to cross the border one evening for a fish meal at a cheap local tavern they knew of. After travelling a few miles into Slovenia, the family were stopped by a group of soldiers and ordered out of the car. The heavily armed men took their coats, seized the car, and drove off, leaving the family stranded on a remote road.

After about an hour the soldiers returned, apologised for the mistake, and gave back the family's possessions including the car. The soldiers warned the family that they should return to Italy immediately.

A few miles down the road, the family noticed a funny smell coming from the back of the car. They pulled over to investigate and were horrified when they discovered two dead bodies inside the boot!

Very frightened, and in a state of panic, the family discarded the bodies by the side of the road, and sped off home as quickly as possible.

The Investigation

In the spring of 1993, this horrific tale spread rapidly throughout Italian towns and villages close to the northern border with Slovenia. It was a time of great political unrest in the ex-Yugoslavian regions, and this UL demonstrates the sense of danger and vulnerability felt amongst Italians living close to the border. The fact that this UL surfaced at a time when Slovenia was no longer at war throws doubt on the professionalism and conduct shown by Slovenian soldiers, portraying them as corrupt and ill-disciplined.

This tale has similarities with such legends as The Body In The Bed (CR1702) and Grandma (CR1703). All the legends have the theme of concealed dead bodies. The main difference is that in Grandma, the discovery of the body would be by an unknown party (the thief), and the sickening find is left to your own imagination.

And Finally...

A version of this tale can be found on the Italian website http://leggende.clab.it. The website has a section written in English which contains extracts from different volumes of *Tuttestorie Magazine*. This particular tale was written by Lucia Veccia, and is titled 'A Hearty Meal into the Ex-Jugoslavia'. The website is well worth a visit, although the English translation is a bit dodgy at times. But who am I to complain – I can't even order a cappuccino in Italy without getting it wrong.

Name:	The Beast of Belgium
Code:	AW1908
Origin:	1973, the author Joe Musser
Status:	False

UNCOVERED

The Legend

The rumour is that the EC has constructed a top secret giant super computer based in Belgium which contains databases full of information on every individual in the world. This giant computer is three stories high and occupies an unknown building in a Belgian city. The computer is solely self-programming, and is used to track every man, woman and child on this planet.

The computer is seen as the work of the Antichrist, and its use to control the global economy will bear the mark of the beast. It is this sinister purpose that has earned the super computer the nickname of the 'Beast'.

The Investigation

This amazing but unbelievable rumour has dominated Christian circles for the last thirty years. The combination of the Christian belief in 'the mark of the beast' and the modern conspiracy theorists' suggestion that a secret global government controls the world economy makes a fascinating fusion of a legend that will not lie down and die.

The idea of a giant super computer that is three stories high was probably more believable when the legend first started back in 1973, but simply doesn't wash in today's silicone world of modern technology. We all know that with the capabilities of modern computers, it wouldn't take a computer of that size to do the task. But as unbelievable as it is, this legend will keep being retold time and time again.

Another flaw is that the computer is supposed to be self-programming. There have been major advances in AI (artificial intelligence) over the last few years, but as far as I am aware it hasn't reached the 'Antichrist' status just yet, so the idea of that kind of technology being around in the 1970s is just a joke. Even if the technology was available, how can you possibly track every human being on the planet?

Admittedly we do seem to be edging that way, with people being tracked using GPS technology and every transaction that is made with a credit or debit card being logged and monitored. In London, cameras are reading and tracking number plates of vehicles that enter the Congestion Charge zone, and CCTV cameras are absolutely everywhere. It's easy to see why people are becoming increasingly paranoid.

However, I still maintain that The Beast Of Belgium is a complete work of fiction. The legend was first recognised on a large scale when the magazine *Christian Life* printed the story in 1976. Soon after, *Christian Life* received a letter from Joe Musser who claimed he had invented the story three years beforehand. Apparently, the story was fabricated for his novel *Behold a Pale Horse* and for the screenplay for the David Wilkerson film *The Rapture*. Joe Musser was shocked that the story was taken as gospel (pardon the pun!) and stated that for three years he had watched the legend being passed around as fact.

The legend was hyped even more by the clever promotional campaign for the movie *The Rapture*. Believable mock newspapers that featured the Beast Of Belgium story were printed and distributed, with hardly anything to suggest that the news stories printed were fiction.

And Finally...

Outside of Christian circles this legend would be scoffed at immediately as a ridiculous conspiracy theory, but certain fundamentalist Christians have a deep-seated mistrust and fear of new technology. This is nothing new, as through the ages Christians have often greeted technological advances as signs of the Last Days. TV, cinema and pop music have all been met with suspicion, even being seen as the work of the Antichrist. Some people believe that computers and the Internet are the proof that signify the Last Days – but not everybody is so fearful; many Christians use these means to reach a broader audience and to 'spread the word'.

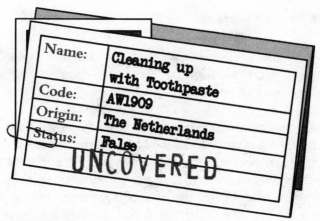

Name:	Cleaning up with Toothpaste
Code:	AW1909
Origin:	The Netherlands
Status:	False

UNCOVERED

The Legend

When an employee of a company barged into the director's office and told him that he had an excellent idea to generate a bigger profit, the director said it had better be a good one… and this was! The company produced toothpaste, and the employee reckoned that he could boost sales by ten per cent. Intrigued, the director asked how the employee proposed to achieve such a task.

Before the employee was willing to share his great idea, he made the director sign an agreement granting him the right to a given annual percentage of the profit for the rest of his life if the idea was used. This was all agreed, and the employee now lives a life of luxury and is worth millions of pounds. So what was this great idea, I hear you ask? Well, it's simple:

Enlarge the hole of the toothpaste tube by ten per cent. The consumers will not notice this change and will squeeze the same length of toothpaste onto their toothbrushes. But because the hole is bigger, they will use more toothpaste and will have to buy new toothpaste tubes more regularly.

The Investigation

In the Netherlands, the term used for ULs is 'broodje aap verhalen', which translates as 'monkey burgers' in English. I collected this rags to riches tale from a Dutch website named Broodje Aap, which was created by Patrick Arink.

Patrick has informed me that he first heard the legend being told in a pub in the early 1990s (if the bloke down the pub told it, it must be true). Another time, he heard the story in a different part of the Netherlands while listening to a conversation on a bus.

This is a typical get-rich-quick tale that most people can relate to as it captures the dream we all have of making it big. After all, if such a simple idea can bring success, why can't it happen to you?

It is also a success story for the small guy. What a great world we live in when low-level employees can out-think the big corporate fat cats with their teams of advisers, big-budget marketing strategies and think tanks. There's hope for all of us!

And Finally...

I am sure I am not the only person to wonder why the Dutch call ULs monkey burgers, and I am sure I was not the first to think that it may be the product of spending too much time in those Amsterdam cafés. Well, I have yet to confirm the meaning, but I do have a feeling that it originates from a legend that a certain fast-food chain substituted monkey meat for beef in their burgers. If anyone has a clearer idea to the true meaning, please let me know.

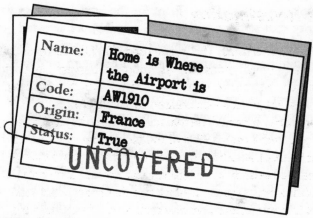

Name:	Home is Where the Airport is
Code:	AW1910
Origin:	France
Status:	True

UNCOVERED

The Legend

A refugee from Iran was stranded at the Charles de Gaulle Airport in Paris for well over a decade. Believe it or not, this is true!

Merhan Karimi Nasseri (nicknamed 'Sir Alfred' by airport staff) was expelled from Iran in 1977 for his vocal political views against the Shah of Iran. He quickly found himself with no home, passport or documents, and with nowhere to go. Over the next few years Alfred desperately sought asylum in seven different European capitals to no avail, then in 1981, four years after he was deported from Iran, he was finally declared a political refugee by the United Nations High Commission in Belgium. With the vital documents he had waited so long to obtain, Alfred set out on his journey with a revived enthusiasm. His destination? England.

At that point, fate dealt another cruel blow to his fortunes. After a long journey to Paris by train, his briefcase was stolen at the railway station, and Alfred arrived in Paris without the important documents he had been issued. Undeterred, Alfred went straight to the Charles de Gaulle Airport in Paris and boarded a plane for London. Customs staff at Heathrow Airport did not greet him with open arms, and without any documents or a passport, they had no choice but to bundle him on the

227

next plane back to Paris. To make the situation even worse, security staff at the Charles de Gaulle Airport arrested Alfred for illegal entry. The French wanted to deport him, but with no documents or passport, they had nowhere to deport him to. Alfred spent the next few years in and out of jail for illegal immigration, before making Terminal One his adopted home.

A human rights lawyer took up the fight for Alfred's rights, but it took years for any progress to be made. Finally, in 1992, a French court ruled that Alfred entered Terminal One as a political refugee and cannot be expelled from it. This was all very well, but the court could not force the French government to allow Alfred to leave the airport onto French soil. The government refused to allow him citizenship in France, and wouldn't provide a transit visa.

Alfred needed to return to Belgium where he had received the original documents, but was unable to do so without a transit visa. The Belgian government were willing to hand Alfred the necessary documents, but he had to claim the papers in person. That's what I call a catch-22 situation.

The legal battles continued, and in 1995 it looked as though Alfred's lawyer had made a breakthrough. Alfred was given permission to enter Belgium to regain his papers, but as always there was a catch. He was allowed to return only if he stayed in Belgium for a year under supervision by a social worker. Unbelievably, Alfred refused, claiming he would only leave Terminal One to travel to Britain.

Finally, in July 1999, Alfred was handed his papers by the Belgian government, making Alfred a free man and allowing him to leave the airport any time he wished. But the tale ends with a pinch of irony, with Alfred still lodging at Terminal One. All those years stranded at the airport must have made Alfred slightly loco, as he no longer wanted to leave. He feels safe in the boundaries of the terminal, and considers the airport staff family.

'Sir Alfred' is still the resident celebrity of the Charles de Gaulle Airport, and receives many cards and letters from well-wishers the world over.

The Investigation

This amazing true story is a great example of bureaucracy gone mad. No wonder the poor man has lost his marbles – he has had to suffer years of slow legal battles and mind-blowing administrative procedures that don't seem to make any sense at all outside the world of law. The Belgian government claimed that they were sympathetic with Sir Alfred's situation, but insisted he had to come and collect the papers he needed in person, knowing full well that he was unable to leave the airport. Then we have the French who didn't want Alfred, but would not supply him with the transit visa he needed to leave the airport and travel to Belgium. This went on for years and years, proving what a crazy world we live in.

The only variation in detail from version to version of this fascinating true tale is the description of how he actually lost his papers in the first place. One article claims that he had sent the papers back to Belgium in a moment of 'folly', while *The Times* claims that he lost the documents while on a ferry. Other articles claim that the documents were taken when he was mugged at a Paris train station, while most agree that the suitcase he was carrying that contained the papers were stolen on a train while Alfred was heading for Paris.

Alfred is now free to leave whenever he wishes, but to the best of my knowledge the airport still remains his home. Why? My guess is that it must be similar to the situation of prisoners who have served a long term in jail. They have spent so long living in a regulated and controlled environment, where they hardly have to think for themselves, that they end up relying on the routine and would feel lost and isolated in the real world and unable to cope. Charles de Gaulle Airport is Alfred's prison, and he has spent too long relying on the kindness of the airport staff to fend for himself. He feels safe at the airport and probably would feel very vulnerable in the outside world.

And Finally...

I bet you are all wondering how Merhan Karimi Nasseri earned the nickname 'Sir Alfred'?

While a refugee, Alfred's quest to enter Britain never dwindled and he applied many times, each time getting turned down. On the immigration application forms there was a space to enter an adopted name of choice; Nasseri wrote Alfred in the box simply because he liked the name. Employees at the Charles de Gaulle Airport learned of this and started calling him Sir Alfred, or just Alfred, and the name stuck.

It is believed that the idea and screenplay of the 2004 film *The Terminal*, starring Tom Hanks and directed by Steven Spielberg, was inspired by Nasseri's story.

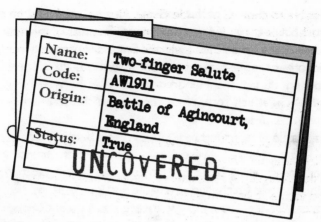

Name:	Two-finger Salute
Code:	AW1911
Origin:	Battle of Agincourt, England
Status:	True

UNCOVERED

The Legend

The two-finger salute is a gesture of defiance and anger used mainly in Britain. The reversed 'V' sign originated from the Battle of Agincourt in 1415, where the successful English used the sign as a symbol of triumph over the defeated French prisoners.

Before the battle, the French anticipated victory, and threatened to cut off three fingers from the right hand of every man they captured. This would ensure that the famous English longbow archers would not be able to draw their bows and would be unable to fight again.

But, against all odds, the English were victorious, and the two-fingered salute was given in a mocking fashion to passing French prisoners to show that they still had all of their fingers.

The Investigation

Although widely used in Britain, the sign would not be recognised in many other countries throughout the world. It is similar to the American gesture of 'giving the finger', and is used in the same vein.

The origin theories of this fascinating legend are based on fact, but the battle during which the sign was first used has long been debated. Most agree that it was the Battle of Agincourt in 1415, but another theory points to Crécy in 1346. It almost certainly happened during the Hundred Years War between England and France, which took place throughout the fourteenth and fifteenth centuries.

The Battle of Agincourt took place when a battle-weary English army led by Henry V were returning home from France after a long and gruelling battle at Harfleur. The French blocked the English route to Calais, and so a battle was inevitable. The French were confident of victory, and were even laughing and joking over a big breakfast before the battle. The English were less confident, and with good reason; the French army had 25,000 men, the English only 6,000.

Henry V made a rousing speech just before the battle commenced, reminding the English archers of the French threat to cut off their fingers. This very thought must have got their adrenalin going, seeing them through the battle, and after victory they mocked the passing French prisoners by sticking up their two fingers to show that they could still draw a bow.

The rest is history.

And Finally...

Many claim the following to be true, but I seriously have my doubts! The longbow used to be made from an English yew tree, and the process of drawing the bow was known as 'plucking the yew'. Not only did the English stick their two fingers up at the French, but also, to let them know that they could still draw a bow, they shouted 'Pluck yew'. Over the years the words have got distorted and the word 'pluck' changed to the similar-sounding 'f' word, with the whole meaning mutating into a sexual reference.

It is also said that the term 'giving the bird', with reference to the one-finger salute, originates from the fact that the arrows used to contain pheasant feathers.

I don't know about you, but I think I will take that with a heavy dosage of salt.

CATEGORY: NETLORE

Netlore is a relatively new subject in UL terms. Ever since skinny, square-eyed nerds have been able to hack into top secret military establishments or unleash a simple computer virus that has the capability to cripple half the world's economy, people are not just apprehensive of this new technology, they are petrified – and who can blame them?

OK – so what have the Internet, James Bond and the space race got in common? They are all products of the Cold War. It is hard to believe that the origins of the Internet started as a glimmer in the eyes of scientists way back in the early 1960s, and was first put into practice in 1969 when four US universities were connected by ARPANET (the Advance Research Projects Agency Network). The whole concept of the Internet was born from the US government's fear of a nuclear attack by the Russians. If America did come under attack, there was a fear that the government's communications network would be disabled and they would not be able to command their military. So in case of such an emergency, the US government decided that information needed to be sent to the military instantly by interconnecting certain positions across the country. Universities were the chosen positions and the government funded the whole project.

In 1973 ARPANET had reached our shores, and connections between the University College in London and the Royal Radar

Establishment in Norway were established. This was the first time that ARPANET had gone international.

Developments were continually made, and the massive boom of personal computers helped the growth of the Internet in the 1980s. With this new popularity came 'hackers', and a great concern over security and privacy arose. This worry was realised on 1 November 1988, when a program called 'Internet Worm' managed to disable ten per cent of the 60,000 Internet hosts.

The ARPANET was finally decommissioned in 1990, leading the way for a new and exciting project called the World Wide Web (WWW). The next few years saw the emergence of the first text-based websites and browsers. Major advances were made in the 1990s, helped by the creation of Gopher (the first point and click means of navigation on the Internet), Mosaic (the first browser), and the creation of HTML (Internet-based computer language).

It is also important to mention that the origins of e-mail were created by Ray Tomlinson way back in 1971, although this important discovery was hardly recognised at the time. So what was the first ever message sent from one computer to another, I hear you ask? Well, it is said to be 'QWERTYUIOP' – hardly the stuff of legends.

So there you have it, the Internet has evolved from the Cold War military and research background into an 'information super highway' playing a major role in our everyday lives. But before the cyber world can start patting itself on the back it must realise that the silicon revolution has brought its own dangers. Pornography is too easily accessed by kids, and the Internet has acted as a springboard for the ever-increasing community of paedophiles. Online banking and e-commerce are most certainly the way forward, but the threat to financial security will always be its Achilles heel. The Western world relies so heavily on this new technology that it is possible for anyone with the means and knowledge to cripple governments and economies with a simple computer virus (e.g. The Love Letter). It is even possible for mass panic to be caused by clever hoaxes like the Good Times Virus (NL6501), resulting in mass hysteria that any terrorist organisation would be proud of.

Fears and anxieties over modern technology have always been a favourite subject matter for folklorists to discuss, but the introduction of the Internet and e-mails has forced the new category of netlore into prominence. Netlore is folklore on speed. Instead of stories getting passed on by word of mouth as is the traditional method, they are spread through the use of e-mail, reaching a global audience almost instantly.

Name:	Good Times Virus
Code:	NL6501
Origin:	1994
Status:	False

UNCOVERED

The Legend: Version 1

IMPORTANT

Please be alerted to a file headed Good Times.

Happy Chanukah to one and all, and take care. If you receive anything by e-mail called 'Good Times', DO NOT read or download this file. It is a new virus on America Online that will cause your hard drive to crash and wipe out its memory. Everyone needs to be informed, so be sure to forward this to your friends and family.

The Legend: Version 2

A friendly warning…

An AOL user has created and put into circulation a new virus of unprecedented destructive power. Well-known viruses such as Airwolf, Stoned and Michaelangelo pale into insignificance when compared to this killer virus, the spawn of a very twisted mind. What separates it from the rest is that it is simply spread by e-mails through the Internet: no file or program exchange is required in order for infection to take place.

The good news is that you can easily identify what is now known as the 'Good Times' virus, because it is always transmitted in the same way – it will arrive in the form of a text e-mail, subject: 'Good Times'. If you receive this file, DO NOT read it. This would result in the file being loaded into the mail server's ASCII buffer, triggering the initialisation and execution of the 'Good Times' virus program.

The virus will then duplicate itself and send copies to everyone who is in your e-mail address book, before erasing your hard drive.

If you receive this e-mail, do not read it or even open it: delete it from your inbox immediately. You can be sure that whoever the virus arrived from has already lost their hard drive to this virus, so warn all your friends of this latest Internet threat.

The Investigation

'Good Times' is the classic computer virus hoax, and it sent mass panic across the English-speaking world when the original version was started back in December 1994.

Experts were quick to denounce the virus threat as a hoax as it was not possible to execute a program by simply opening an e-mail. This did little to stem the panic, and large companies such as Citibank, Texas Instruments and AT&T fell for it hook, line, and sinker, with IT staff cluttering up employees' inboxes even further with desperate warning messages. Even American government agencies were affected, such as the Department of Defence and NASA.

The spread of the hoax has been blamed on business management personnel who did possess the knowledge to spot that it was a hoax, but had the ability to spread it on a wide scale very rapidly.

Version 1 is a representation of one of the original e-mail messages that were sent out in 1994. As you can see, the original was short, sweet and to the point. You will also notice that the seasonal greeting 'Happy Chanukah' is included in the warning. 'Chanukah' is the Jewish holiday for the festival of lights, and this dates the e-mail to late November, early December.

Version 2 is a later version, and probably the version most commonly read. The message is a lot more long-winded and goes into greater detail on the technicality of the virus.

No one knows for sure who actually started the hoax, and we probably never will. The date most commonly associated with the original Good Times virus is 2 December 1994. One copy was found with the date being 29 November 1994, although this date could have easily been forged.

And Finally...

A computer virus is a patch or snippet of computer code that first infects the host program, and then starts to perform its task. The virus usually corrupts the program into performing other tasks that result in the virus being spread to other programs. Viruses are usually spread to other computers by infected programs on floppy disks, CD ROMs, or on attachment programs by e-mail.

You could compare the hoax itself, or indeed any UL, to a virus. The hoaxes are spread rapidly via e-mails and can cause as much panic and paranoia as real viruses. Instead of a snippet of code infecting a computer and making it perform tasks, the hoax manipulates the reader into sending out other hoax warning e-mails.

Name:	Budweiser Frogs Screensaver
Code:	NL6502
Origin:	1997
Status:	False

UNCOVERED

The Legend: Version 1

VIRUS ALERT!

=====================

THIS IS A NEW VIRUS. A TWISTED PRANKSTER IS SENDING OUT A VERY CUTE SCREENSAVER {{THE BUD FROGS}}. ONCE DOWNLOADED, IT WILL ERASE EVERYTHING ON YOUR HARD DRIVE!!

WHATEVER YOU DO, DO NOT DOWNLOAD THIS SCREENSAVER!! IT WAS FIRST REPORTED ON 13/05/97.

FORWARD THIS INFO TO EVERYONE IN YOUR ADDRESS BOOK...
THIS IS WHAT THE SCREENSAVER PROGRAM LOOKS LIKE:

File: BUDSAVER.EXE

The Legend: Version 2

This morning I received the following warning from a reliable source. Please read it carefully.

IMPORTANT

There is a new virus in circulation by e-mail offering a free screensaver with the file name BUDDYLST.SIP.

If you receive this e-mail, DO NOT OPEN IT!!!!!

If you do, your hard drive will be wiped clean. Not only that, but the person who sent you the e-mail will have access to your login information. We believe this highly destructive new virus began circulating yesterday.

We need to act now to block this virus so please forward this e-mail to everyone in your address book. AOL, Demon and BT Internet have all confirmed the danger this virus poses. As yet no anti-virus program has been developed.

Do not ignore this e-mail: be sure to forward this information to everyone you know.

The Investigation

Long before 'WASSUPP' was shouted down phones at every opportunity, Budweiser had a successful marketing campaign with the Budweiser frogs. The unlikely amphibian stars were an instant success, and in 1996, a free downloadable screensaver of the Bud frogs proved to be popular. But, of course, there is always someone who has to try and spoil it for everyone.

In 1997, with the free download growing ever more popular, some prankster (or a word to that effect!) decided to try and burst Budweiser's bubble with a virus hoax.

The hoax was spread like wildfire via e-mail, and was a little harder to spot as a hoax than its predecessors as it claimed that the virus was contained in the executable file, rather than the actual text of the e-mail (which cannot be done).

Version 1 is taken from one of the earliest versions that were being sent out in 1997. The warning is short and very primitive. The amount of exclamation points used to overstate a point made it easy pickings for hoax-busters.

Version 2 is a later version and, like so many ULs, has an extra twist. Not only will your hard drive be wiped, but also the person who sent you the virus would have access to your name and password via the Internet. Version 2 is a little more complex, and so maybe a little more believable than Version 1.

And Finally...

Computer virus hoaxes are a real menace and can achieve as much damage as a real virus. They may not wipe your hard drive, but the real effects can be just as devastating. The fear of a virus causes a loss of confidence as well as bad publicity, and this can hit companies and individuals hard.

There are plenty of antivirus websites on the Internet that can inform you whether a virus warning is real or just a hoax. These websites advise that the best way to stamp out a virus hoax is to have a better awareness and simply not forward the warnings to others. If only it was that simple.

The moral of the story is: don't panic, but do be careful when opening any executable file contained within an e-mail, especially if you don't know the person who sent it.

Name:	Racist Word
Code:	NL6503
Origin:	Unknown
Status:	False

UNCOVERED

The Legend

It is claimed that Microsoft are part of a global racist conspiracy spreading its messages of hate throughout the world. The proof has not been hidden in a piece of complex programming, or discovered by a sophisticated hacker. In fact, it hasn't been hidden at all and can easily be accessed by anyone: the proof can be found in the Thesaurus function of MS Word.

Type the following sentence in MS Word and highlight it:

'I hope Microsoft will rule the world.'

Now enter the Thesaurus function and you will see:

'I should say so.'

It gets worse! Now type in:

'I'd like all gays dead.'

The Thesaurus responds:

'I'll drink to that.'

And if that wasn't bad enough, type in:

'Kill all Jews.'

The response is:

'Kill in cold blood.'

If you have MS Word on your computer, try this, and discover the horrifying truth.

The Investigation

This piece of netlore is one of many that can be categorised as part of the growing 'anti Bill Gates' movement, and there are plenty of those who are opposed to the geek turned good. Bill Gates is the focus of a barrage of legends that either targets him personally or his company, Microsoft. Bill Gates has been accused of everything from being an anti-Semitic devil worshipper to being part of a global conspiracy to rule the world. A bit dramatic, maybe, but it shows the depth of hate that people harbour and the lengths that they will go to to tarnish the name of one of the richest men in the world.

So, is there any truth in this claim about the Thesaurus in MS Word? Well, I tried these sentences out on my trusty version of Word and the Thesaurus certainly didn't come out with the alleged comments. Although this does not mean that earlier versions didn't, and the language setting may have to be in US English. I typed in the following using Word 2002, and it may be different with newer Word versions.

When I typed in 'I hope Microsoft will rule the world', my

Thesaurus came up with 'I imagine', which could be seen as a similar response, but when I looked down the list I also found 'ill-advised', which is contradictory to the theory.

I then typed in the sentence 'I'd like all gays dead', and one of the suggestions of the MS Word Thesaurus was 'idolize', but another was 'I don't know'.

However, with the sentence 'Kill all Jews', one of the suggestions was indeed 'Kill in cold blood'!

It is easy to manipulate a Thesaurus list for your own purposes when looking up a particular phrase. Taking one phrase or word out of context gives us no more than circumstantial and selective evidence, and therefore cannot be used as verified proof of the claims made in this UL. In fact, all the Thesaurus is doing is returning in alphabetical order everyday words and expressions similar to the one typed. Instead of inserting 'I hope Microsoft will rule the world', you could insert 'I hope Bill Gates will eat dung for breakfast' and the Thesaurus response would be the same. There is nothing sinister about this so-called 'phenomenon' at all.

However, although the Thesaurus responses above contain no intentional malice, the same cannot be said of when Microsoft contracted out the programming of Windows 95 for the Chinese market. A few Taiwan Chinese programmers took this as a chance to spread their political hatred of the Chinese leaders to the whole of the Chinese market, and inserted phrases that labelled the Beijing leaders 'Communist bandits'. Other suggestions for finishing sentences urged loyal Taiwanese to 'take to the mainland'. Microsoft quickly realised what had been done and promptly removed all the offensive phrases from the system, thereby avoiding a diplomatic crisis.

And Finally...

As an experiment I typed the sentence 'I hope Microsoft will rule the world' onto a Lotus WordPro document (a rival of Microsoft), and checked out the Thesaurus for the response.

The result was quite surprising but in any case honest: the response was, 'I think not' and 'I don't think so'. I am sure that's just a coincidence, aren't you?

Name:	The Broken Cup-holder
Code:	NL6504
Origin:	1996
Status:	Undecided

UNCOVERED

The Legend: Version 1

Logged conversation from a Novell Netware technical support centre:

Caller: Hi, is this Tech Support?

Technician: It sure is. My name is Jerry. Can I help you?

Caller: I only bought my PC last month and already the cup-holder on it is broken. It's well within the warranty period so I was hoping you could tell me how to get it replaced.

Technician: I'm not sure I understood you – did you say a cup-holder?

Caller: Yeah, the one that pops out the front of the computer.

Technician: I must admit, I am a little confused here. Where did you get the cup-holder from, was it part of a promotional package? Can you see any reference code on it?

Caller: It was already installed on the computer when I bought it. There is a code – it just has '4X' on it.

The technician started to laugh and had to press 'Mute' on his phone. The caller had been using the CD ROM loader as a cup-holder!

The Legend: Version 2

The following is a taped conversation from an English-based technical support centre.

Technician: Hi, you are through to technical support. How may I be of assistance?

Caller: Hello, I am hoping you can help me. My computer is only a week old and the cup-holder on the front has broken.

Technician: What do you mean when you say cup-holder?

Caller: You know, the little drinks tray that slides out from the front of the computer.

Technician: That's strange! Is the cup-holder a customised addition?

Caller: No, it was already installed when I bought the computer. It says '4X' on the front.

At this moment, it dawns on the technician what has happened and he bursts out laughing – the 'cup-holder' that the caller is referring to is actually the CD ROM player.

The Investigation

Yes, believe it or not, there really are people out there who are that stupid. There are many technical support stories, but this one is probably the most famous. Although this is widely stated as being a true incident, I have yet to see any verification of the authenticity of the legend. The recent versions (such as Version 2) are normally situated in England, but company names are not usually given. Only in the older versions (such as Version 1) are the names of the companies included, and they are usually large computer companies such as Apple or Novell Netware. The origins of the story are unclear, but Version 1 is the earliest I have found, and it is a representation of an e-mail that was sent on the 19 June 1996.

The Broken Cup-holder legend justifies the concern of a section of society that new technology is complex and unfathomable. Some people should just stick to a typewriter.

And Finally...

One of my favourite technical support legends travelling the e-mail circuit is a recorded message left on an answer machine. A customer complains that his pointer is in the middle of the screen and he is unable to move it left because his mouse is on the left edge of the pad, and if he moves it any more the mouse will go off the pad. Enough said.

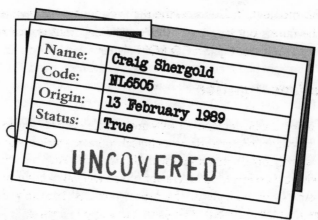

Name:	Craig Shergold
Code:	NL6505
Origin:	13 February 1989
Status:	True

UNCOVERED

The Legend

Craig Shergold is a seven-year-old boy from Carshalton, Surrey, who is dying from an inoperable brain tumour. It is his wish to enter *The Guinness Book of Records* for the largest number of 'get well soon' cards received by one person.

Please find it in your heart to spare a moment of your time to help fulfil Craig's wish.

Please send your card to the following address:

(**address supplied**)

P.S. Please pass this message on to all your friends and relatives.

The Investigation

Although the legend of Craig Shergold is extremely well padded around the edges, it is based on a true story. The truth is that Craig Shergold was actually a nine-year-old boy when he was diagnosed with cancer (following a brain tumour) on 13 February 1989. Craig received many 'get well soon' cards from friends and relatives, and it was his doctor's idea to campaign for *The Guinness Book of Records*. At that stage Craig had only received 200 cards, but after his plight had made headline news in the *Mirror* and *The Sun*, the cards began pouring in. It is estimated that by October 1989, 200,000 cards a week were being sent. This was a major problem as the special sorting room set up at Sutton United Football Club could only handle about 60,000 a week.

The record to beat stood at just over a million cards, and a boy named Mario Morby from Leicester held that record. On 16 November 1989, Mario's record was smashed, and still the cards kept piling in for Craig.

In 1991, American billionaire John W. Kluge flew Craig to the University of Virginia Medical Centre for an operation to remove the brain tumour. After the successful operation, Craig and his family thanked everyone who had sent Craig a card but appealed for no more cards to be sent so that they could live a normal life. Mainly thanks to chain e-mails the appeal was in vain, and the cards just kept pouring in. One source has estimated that Craig has received over a hundred million cards to date. I am surprised that Clinton Cards did not open up a special 'Get Well Soon Craig' section in their shops!

Of course, with legends the facts can get a little blurred around the edges, and the Craig Shergold legend is no exception. Craig's surname has also been Sherwood, Sherhold, Shargold, and Shirgold. The county of Surrey has been changed to Surry, or Surney. Carshalton is also known as Charshalton, Carshaltonn or Carshelton. Some chain letters even claim that Craig lives in Canada, or Virginia, USA.

And Finally...

The heart-warming story of Craig Shergold has long been obscured by legend, and the results have been damaging, wasting time and resources for charities and organisations for the needy. The latest chain letters urge readers to forward their cards to the Make-A-Wish Foundation, Virginia, USA. The foundation has had to add a page debunking such legends on their website. They state that all cards received for Craig Shergold will be forwarded straight to a recycling centre.

Name:	Internet Clean-up Day
Code:	NL6506
Origin:	1996
Status:	False

UNCOVERED

The Legend

Subject: Internet Clean-up Day

*** Attention ***

Be prepared: the time for the annual Internet Clean-up is drawing near.

In order to eliminate broken links, unused www domain names and spam that is cluttering up the Internet, the Internet will be closed down for a period of 24 hours to allow us to clean it.

The cleaning process will commence at 12:01 a.m. GMT on 15 February and end at 12:01 a.m. GMT on 16 February (this time period has been carefully chosen for best damage limitation to the business environment). Five powerful international search engines will be put into action to search the web and destroy any unwanted data and spam they find.

Important: You must protect your data by following these steps: Disconnect your PC and any networked PC from the Internet.

Shut down all servers and modems, or disconnect from the Internet.

Ensure that any disks or hard drives are disconnected from the Internet.

DO NOT connect any computer to the Internet in any way.

We apologise for any inconvenience this may cause, but are sure you will reap the benefits of a more efficient and faster Internet.

Thank you for your understanding in this matter.

*** Signature Removed ***

The Investigation

E-mail circulars about Internet Clean-up Day such as the one given above started circulating in 1996. Since then, it has become a yearly joke, and a legend in its own right. The annual hoax usually claims to be a public service announcement, and states that on a certain day the Internet will be cleaned of all junk mail, bookmarks and unused files.

And Finally...

Most versions ask you to turn off the computer and disconnect any links to the Internet, but one version stated that all you had to do was put a cloth over the computer for the day.

Even though this hoax reappears year after year, there are still people out there stupid enough to fall for it. There is NO Internet

Clean-up Day, and if you don't have broadband, the Internet will still be as slow as ever. This UL feeds on the gullibility of people and exploits the fact that some users have little knowledge or understanding of the Internet. A good example of this is that a friend of mine used to press what looked like a standard light switch on the wall each time she was about to use the Internet. When I questioned her on why she did this, she told me that she had seen her dad do it before he had gone online. When I quizzed her dad about the switch he just laughed and told me it had nothing to do with the Internet – it just switched the security light on and off outside the house and he would make a habit of checking it. At least everyone knows when she is online: you can see the light from right down the street!

Name:	Aircraft Maintenance
Code:	NL6507
Origin:	Unknown
Status:	Undecided

UNCOVERED

The Legend

After every flight, pilots complete a gripe sheet which conveys the mechanical problems encountered with the aircraft during the flight that need repair or correction.

The form is a piece of paper that the pilot fills in and then the mechanics read and correct the problems. They then respond in writing on the lower half of the form what remedial action was taken and the pilot reviews the gripe sheet before the next flight.

Here are some actual logged maintenance complaints and problems:

P = The problem logged by the pilot.
S = The solution and action taken by the mechanics.

P: Left inside main tyre almost needs replacement.
S: Almost replaced left inside main tyre.

P: Test flight OK, except autoland very rough.
S: Autoland not installed on this aircraft.

P: Something loose in cockpit.
S: Something tightened in cockpit.

P: Dead bugs on windshield.
S: Live bugs on back-order.

P: Autopilot in altitude-hold mode produces a 200 fpm descent.
S: Cannot reproduce problem on ground.

P: Evidence of leak on right main landing gear.
S: Evidence removed.

P: DME volume unbelievably loud.
S: DME volume set to more believable level.

P: Aircraft handles funny.
S: Aircraft warned to straighten up, fly right and be serious.

The Investigation

This is an e-mail that I received in October 2002. This 'list' arrangement is an instantly recognisable format in ULs that are spread by e-mail, and is used to document everything from computer helpline conversations, doctors' notes on patients and quotes from the courtroom to excuses from parents for students, quotes from accident report forms and signs and menus translated into poor English by foreigners. I could go on and on reeling off the categories, and easily have enough material for a large book on this kind of UL alone.

Most of the material that is circulated via e-mails today could have been found sitting on top of a fax machine's intray ten years ago. Similarly, it could have been found pinned up on a company's bulletin board or printed in a newsletter thirty to forty years before that. In other words, this is a typical 'office water cooler conversation' that reproduces and recycles the same information but with variations. This is why I consider the 'lists' as ULs.

And Finally...

Here are a few examples of 'list' legends:

Absence notes for students from their parents:
Please excuse Fiona from being absent yesterday. She was in bed with Gramps.
My son is under the doctor's care and should not take PE. Please execute him.

Doctors' notes:
The patient refused an autopsy.
The patient has no past history of suicides.
She is numb from her toes down.

Lawyers' questions in court:
Was that the same nose you broke as a child?
How long have you been a French-Canadian?
Was it you or your brother who was killed in the war?

Name:	Foreign Signs
Code:	NL6508
Origin:	Unknown
Status:	Undecided

UNCOVERED

The Legend

The following signs have been found in various locations, using the English language somewhat creatively…

At a Budapest zoo:
PLEASE DO NOT FEED THE ANIMALS. IF YOU HAVE ANY SUITABLE FOOD, GIVE IT TO THE GUARD ON DUTY.

Doctor's office, Rome:
SPECIALIST IN WOMEN AND OTHER DISEASES.

Hotel, Acapulco:
THE MANAGER HAS PERSONALLY PASSED ALL THE WATER SERVED HERE.

Sign in men's toilet in Japan:
TO STOP LEAK TURN COCK TO THE RIGHT.

In a city restaurant:
OPEN SEVEN DAYS A WEEK, AND WEEKENDS TOO.

A sign seen on an automatic hand dryer:
DO NOT ACTIVATE WITH WET HANDS.

In a Pumwani maternity ward:
NO CHILDREN ALLOWED.

Sign in Japanese public bath:
FOREIGN GUESTS ARE REQUESTED NOT TO PULL COCK IN TUB.

Tokyo hotel's rules and regulations:
GUESTS ARE REQUESTED NOT TO SMOKE OR DO OTHER DISGUSTING BEHAVIOURS IN BED.

In a Tokyo bar:
SPECIAL COCKTAILS FOR THE LADIES WITH NUTS.

In a Bangkok temple:
IT IS FORBIDDEN TO ENTER A WOMAN EVEN A FOREIGNER IF DRESSED AS A MAN.

Hotel in Japan:
YOU ARE INVITED TO TAKE ADVANTAGE OF THE CHAMBERMAID.

Airline ticket office, Copenhagen:
WE TAKE YOUR BAGS AND SEND THEM IN ALL DIRECTIONS.

The Investigation

This is an e-mail that I received on 13 December 2001, and is a good example of many that I have received over the last few years. Foreign mangling of the English language has always provided much amusement for the English-speaking world. English is a dominant language in the world, and a bad grasp of this complex language can lead to some very humorous translations.

And Finally...

Of course, the importance of understanding the language you wish to communicate in can work both ways, as Nike found out to their embarrassment. You may recall a Nike advert with Samburu tribesmen crossing Kenya, with one of the tribe speaking his native language. The subtitle at the bottom of the screen reads, 'Just Do It!'

But the tribesman was not as happy with his trainers as everyone thought, because what he actually said was, 'I don't want these. Give me big shoes!'

This was not noticed until a couple of weeks into the advertising campaign. Then, to Nike's great embarrassment, the mistake was plastered across every national American newspaper. Some may say that this is another great example of a large corporate company not paying enough attention to detail and ending up with egg on their face. A little research was all that was needed, and if they thought that no one in their audience would notice a mistake they were very foolish. Within the large and multi-cultured society that is America, someone was bound to speak the Maa language.

CATEGORY: 9/11

The events of September 11th 2001 fatefully changed the skyline of New York. When the Al-Qaeda terrorists decided to use human bombs to cause maximum damage and fatalities, a new evil of global terrorism was brought onto the world stage. Out of the smouldering smoke of 'Ground Zero' a new era was dawning, and the world would never be the same again. 9/11 affected many people from different countries and religions, and these callous acts sent out a cold shiver that stretched across the four corners of the earth. World views and politics have been and continue to be reshaped forever.

It came as no surprise that in one of the bleakest hours of modern history, ULs poured out of the gaping wound from the offset. Legends that focus on 9/11 offend and appal many people and can be viewed as disrespectful and insensitive, but, like jokes, these legends can be seen as part of a healing process in the wake of a tragedy. The tales contain controversy, conspiracy, humour and sinister predictions, all trying to make sense of a situation that most of us simply cannot comprehend.

The ULs surrounding the events of 9/11 are a very important reflection of the fears and thoughts that are rife in the aftermath of the tragedy. They are also being used as a propaganda tool in the fight against terrorism, mirroring the use of ULs in any war. It would take a huge book to cover even half of the legends surrounding the events of 9/11, and new ones are surfacing on a daily basis. Some of the ULs out there are in bad taste and I have been very selective in deciding which ones to include.

The most controversial UL I have tackled in this category has to be Pentagon Attack (WT9807). This conspiracy theory asks questions about the official version given that an aircraft crashed into the Pentagon on 9/11. I have investigated each one of the questions in turn and reported the findings. Don't try and read this one last thing at night.

The Birmingham Warning (WT9808) deals with a subject much closer to home, while you computer club nerds will know all about the Wingdings Conspiracy (WT9802). Bill Gates again – give the bloke a break!

After any tragic event people wonder what they could have done to prevent it. Some seek refuge in the theory that it was 'fate' and it was 'meant to be'. This line of thinking is often backed up by prediction theories. In the aftermath of 9/11 many of these theories emerged, ranging from a prediction in a $20 note (WT9805) to old favourite Nostradamus (WT9803), who apparently foresaw everything from the Great Fire of London and both World Wars to the eerie prophecy that I will have scrambled eggs for my breakfast next Thursday (or did I misread that one?).

And for those of you who have fond memories of the children's TV favourite *Sesame Street*, you will be horrified to hear that Bert has been linked to Osama Bin Laden. You don't believe me? Check out Bert Is Evil (WT9801), and you will see what I mean. Most of the legends in this section have to be seen to be believed, and if you go to the Project 2067 website (www. project2067.com), everything will be explained.

There are certain events in history that get engraved in the memory of people throughout the world. People say that they will always remember what they were doing the exact moment that they heard that JFK had been shot, that man had first landed on the moon, or that Princess Diana had tragically died in a car accident. You will probably always remember what you were doing when events unfolded on the fateful day of September 11th 2001.

Name:	Bert is Evil
Code:	WT9801
Origin:	October 2001
Status:	True

UNCOVERED

The Legend

Sesame Street's Bert can be seen peering over the shoulder of Osama Bin Laden in posters used by Al-Qaeda supporters, protesting against American-led attacks on the Taliban regime in Afghanistan.

The Investigation

Remarkably this is true: the familiar face of lovable Bert can be seen side by side with the world's most notorious terrorist leader, Osama Bin Laden. So, how exactly did this happen?

It was all started by a man named Dino Ignacio, who set up his humorous website as part of a long-running joke claiming that Bert is evil. To prove this, Bert was inserted side by side with the world's most notorious evil figures throughout history. The Bert Is Evil website reached cult status with many copycat sites being started up.

But how did this photo come to appear on protester posters that were printed in Bangladesh? Mostafa Kamal, the production manager of Azad Products who made the posters, reveals the answer. Apparently he found the image on the Internet and included it on the 2,000 posters he printed, not realising that Bert was there. Mostafa stated that he would not include the image on the next poster design.

Shortly after the Bert and Bin Laden image was used on the protesters' posters, Dino Ignacio closed the official Bert Is Evil website. Dino claimed that the cult had grown too big and too close to reality. Bert Is Evil had become too commercialised and had achieved a much greater platform of awareness than Dino had wanted. In other words, it had become more than just a joke. Dino claims that *Sesame Street* played a major part in his childhood, and now that the Bert Is Evil cult had reached the mass media, he didn't wish to have any part in damaging the image of Bert for the children. Dino has appealed to all the copycat sites to follow suit.

And Finally...

The photographs of the poster at anti-US rallies were printed in newspapers throughout the world, and many theories of why the Bert image was inserted on the posters were circulating. One theory was that the CIA had secretly sabotaged the poster's design by inserting the image of Bert next to Osama Bin Laden. The aim of this propaganda coup was to mock the Taliban by using Bert as a symbol of Western commercialism and freedom.

By using the UL code you can view the picture of the poster by visiting the Project 2067 website at www.project2067.com.

Name:	**Wingdings Conspiracy**
Code:	**WT9802**
Origin:	**1992**
Status:	**False**

UNCOVERED

The Legend: Version 1

Follow the instructions below to uncover a sinister conspiracy involving the Wingdings font that may suggest some kind of link between Microsoft and 9/11.

First type the following in capital letters: NYC (short for New York City).

Highlight the text and change the font size to 72.

Highlight and change the font to 'Webdings' – the results are interesting!

Now change the font to 'Wingdings' – even more interesting!

The Legend: Version 2

The flight number of one of the planes that flew into the World Trade Center was Q33NY.

Open a new Word document and type 'Q33NY' in capital letters.

Highlight the text and enlarge it to size 48.

Change the font style to 'Wingdings'.

You will be amazed!

The Investigation

First of all, for those with the means to do so, I recommend that you actually try the above examples for yourselves. For the rest of you, here is what all the fuss is about:

NYC in Webdings:

NYC in Wingdings:
👤✡👆

Q33NY in Wingdings:

✈📄📄👤✡

The Wingdings and the Webdings fonts replace letters with graphic icons. Wingdings has been around a lot longer than Webdings, and first had the conspiracy theorists wetting their pants in 1992 with the 'NYC' hidden meaning. Back then Microsoft were being accused of being anti-Semitic, with the sign being interpreted as 'death to all Jews'. With the skull and crossbones representing death and the Star of David representing Jews, the theory was sort of plausible and even had the *New York Post* giving it headline news status. Microsoft denied all the allegations and put the secret message down to nothing but a coincidence.

Since the events of 9/11 the secret message is seen as a prediction and has taken on a completely different meaning, with the emphasis being on the terrorist attacks on New York City.

The Webdings version of 'NYC' is probably less of a coincidence, and probably was devised to mock the conspiracy theorists who had too much time on their hands and were bound to seek more hidden meanings. The Webdings version can be interpreted as 'I love New York'.

Finally, we will look at the eerie interpretation of flight Q33NY, which according to the e-mails is the flight number of one of the planes that crashed into the World Trade Center. With a little imagination (the two pieces of paper being the two towers) the Wingdings images certainly portray the scene of that particular act of terrorism. That is apart from one major flaw; there was no such flight number as Q33NY. The actual flight numbers of the two aircrafts that crashed into the World Trade Center are American Airlines Flight 11, and United Airlines Flight 175. No eerie prediction here, just good old-fashioned bending of the truth.

And Finally...

With the entire phobia surrounding the millennium, in 1999 a new Wingdings prophetic theory was born. Worries over the 'millennium bug' (computers unable to cope with the date format) and hype over the Nostradamus predictions (not to mention Prince!) meant 1999 was a turbulent time and people were heading for the hills. Perfect ground for ULs, and they didn't disappoint. It was pointed out that MILLENNIUM in the Wingdings font translates in the following way:

💣☀✌☹☻☜♐♀♐✌✝💣☀

In 1999, this was seen as a prediction and therefore pretty scary stuff, which heightened the fears and hype that shrouded the turn of the millennium. Of course, nothing happened – apart from many hangovers, that is.

Name:	The Nostradamus Predictions
Code:	WT9803
Origin:	September 11th 2001
Status:	False

UNCOVERED

The Legend: Version 1

'In the year of the new century and nine months,
From the sky will come a great King of Terror…
The sky will burn at forty-five degrees.
Fire approaches the great new city…

In the city of York there will be a great collapse,
2 twin brothers torn apart by chaos
While the fortress falls the great leader will succumb
Third big war will begin when the big city is burning'

NOSTRADAMUS

The Legend: Version 2

Subject: Re: Nostradamus

Century 6, Quatrain 97

'Two steel birds will fall from the sky on the Metropolis. The sky
will burn at forty-five degrees latitude.

(New York City lies between 40 and 45 degrees.)
Fire approaches the great new city.

Immediately a huge, scattered flame leaps up.
Within months, rivers will flow with blood.
The undead will roam Earth for little time.'

The Legend: Version 3

'In the City of God there will be a great thunder,
Two brothers torn apart by chaos, while the fortress endures,
The great leader will succumb,
The third big war will begin when the big city is burning'

Nostradamus 1654

The Investigation

Did Nostradamus actually predict the terrorist atrocities on New York City on September 11th 2001? The simple answer is no. For those of you who do not know who the hell Nostradamus is (shame on you), I will give a brief lesson in history before continuing. Nostradamus was a French astrologer born in 1503, and is credited for predicting everything from the Great Fire of London and the Great Plague to the rise and fall of Adolf Hitler and World War Two, and ultimately it is widely believed that he has predicted the end of the world. Most of these predictions have come from a collection of prophecies published in 1555 called the Centuries, and each prediction is told in a separate four-line rhyming verse called a quatrain. The predictions are very vague and are usually open for interpretation, and therefore misinterpretation. It is believed that Nostradamus relied heavily on occult divination and horoscopes to enter deep trances that revealed his predictions; this led to his prophecies being condemned by the Catholic Church Congregation in 1781. Although his prophecies have caused much controversy and have caught the imagination of many over the years, he was also known as a pioneer in alternative medicines and treatment for the plague outbreak in 1546–47. History lesson finished.

Version 1 is one of the most common and believable out of all the versions. The only problem with this, as with all the others, is that Nostradamus never actually made this prediction. Instead, it has been made up of snippets of different quatrains and pieced together like a jigsaw. In one quatrain Nostradamus did actually write that 'The sky will burn at forty-five degrees latitude, Fire approaches the new city'. New York is positioned between 40 and 41 degrees latitude, and not at 45 as it has been claimed. Some may argue that the 'forty-five' could actually mean 40.5, and that would be a pretty accurate position. The main flaw in that theory is that metric and decimal places were unheard of in the days of Nostradamus, and so would not be written in that manner. 'Fire approaches the new city' is more likely to refer to Villeneuve-sur-Lot in France. Villeneuve means new city, and it is positioned at 45 degrees latitude.

Version 2 has similarities to Version 1, but contains the extra punch of 'Two steel birds will fall from the sky on the Metropolis', and of course 'Within months, rivers will flow with blood. The undead will roam Earth for little time.' As for the undead roaming the earth, I think that the hoaxer should either cut down on their caffeine intake or stop watching those old Hammer Horror movies!

For someone who died in 1566, I find it astounding that Nostradamus managed to write the quatrain illustrated in Version 3 in the year 1654! With these facts it doesn't exactly take much to debunk this version of the legend, but what is unusual is that its origins can be clearly traced. The fabricated quatrain was originally created in 1997 by Neil Marshal, a student of Brock University in

Canada, and was printed as part of a web page essay. The idea was to point out how a fabricated prophecy can be created by using deliberately vague terms, and interpreted as a prediction of most of the world's cataclysmic events. Ironic, methinks!

And Finally...

This UL is a classic example of how people cling onto false presumptions, no matter how ludicrous, to try and make sense of a surreal situation. It is common that after any catastrophe people take reassurance in whatever way they can, and believing that it has already been mapped out in God's great plan helps unravel the mystery of the situation.

Nostradamus is known throughout the world, but whether his predictions are credible is debatable. He has thousands of supporters worldwide, but many believe that his quatrains are too vague and general, and that they can be associated with most of the great events throughout history. I have no doubt that this debate will continue to the end of time, which apparently Nostradamus has also predicted.

Name:	The Starbucks Outrage
Code:	WT9804
Origin:	September 11th 2001
Status:	True

UNCOVERED

The Legend

On the fateful morning of September 11th 2001, rescue workers for the Brooklyn-based Midwood Ambulance Service – who were helping victims of the terrorist attack – asked at a local Starbucks café for water for the victims. The rescue workers received three crates of bottled water, followed by a bill for $130! The shocked rescue workers had to dig deep and settle the bill out of their own pockets.

The Investigation

So far, we have experienced many ULs that target big corporations with false accusations (e.g. Kentucky Fried Rat – FD3301), but this shocking tale is disturbingly 100 per cent true.

Not only did Starbucks charge $130 as detailed above, the company also completely ignored all calls and e-mails from ambulance officials who were concerned that their rescue workers had been overcharged. One caller who phoned the 'Contact Us' telephone number on Starbucks website was rudely told that it simply could not have happened, and was then thanked for his call.

Starbucks did eventually apologise for the outrage in the form of a personal call by the company's president Orin Smith, and a handwritten cheque to the Midwood Ambulance Service president Al Rapisarda for the amount of $130. The apology was sincere, but was only made after the whole affair became public and had received a great deal of media coverage (mainly thanks to the persistent reporting of a Seattle journalist). The damage had already been done.

The greed of one manager at the Battery Park Plaza Starbucks should not overshadow the fact that Starbucks donated free coffee and gifts to victims and rescue workers in the days following the attack. Starbucks also officially closed for a day in respect for the victims of the terrorist atrocity, and donated $1 million to the September 11th Fund.

And Finally...

Obviously not reading the manual *How to Win Friends and Influence People*, Starbucks unbelievably made another public relations gaffe following the events of September 11th. The storm was caused by advertising posters that had been erected on the walls of all the Starbucks outlets in the USA and Canada. The offending poster was for their brand of Tazo Citrus drinks, and showed two of the drinks standing side by side on grass, photographed from a perspective that made them seem disproportionately large (which could be seen as representing the twin towers), with a dragonfly flying towards the drinks. The slogan of the poster was 'Collapse into cool', and it is that word 'collapse' that probably made the final link of all the visual images to the collapse of the Twin Towers in the public's mind. During a sensitive time, this campaign was appallingly insensitive. Starbucks claimed that the advert was part of a long-running campaign, but other companies aborted any inappropriate campaigns with respect to the sensitivity of the moment, and movies that contained topical material even had their release dates delayed.

Name:	The $20 Prediction
Code:	WT9805
Origin:	4 May 2002
Status:	True

UNCOVERED

The Legend

INCREDIBLE THINGS HAPPEN IN AMERICA...

1. Take a $20 bill and fold it in half lengthways.
2. Now fold it again, as shown.
3. Finally, fold the other end as shown and you should be able to see the PENTAGON on fire!!
4. Keep the note folded and turn it over to reveal... The Twin Towers ablaze.

What a strange coincidence! By simply folding a $20 note you can uncover an eerie premonition of the 9/11 attacks!!

The Investigation

This is a clever e-mail that I received on 21 August 2002, almost a year after the terrorist attacks on America. You can see the pictures illustrating how to fold the note at www.project2067.com. If you look carefully at the notes, you may be able to see the web address http://www.testinadivitello.it/. With a little research I have discovered that the original version comes from the website www.allbrevard.net.

The website claims that one of their 'web guys' discovered this amazing coincidence while at a party on 4 May 2002. A web page was created on the 9 May with the idea of sharing this find with friends. It was thought that only a dozen people would ever see the page but this proved to be a vast miscalculation. Ten days later the hit counter had gone over the million mark, and now the web page has been viewed over two million times.

The original web page called this a coincidence, and that is all it is. This coincidental discovery of images portraying the 9/11 attacks was made by folding a $20 bill into different segments, but the art of folding notes and labels to find amusing pictures and messages has been a popular pastime for many years.

And Finally...

The US Treasury redesigned the present-day $20 bill in 1998, and the folding of older notes will not achieve the same results.

I have classed this UL as true, but just to clarify, I am referring to the results of folding the note and not the actual prediction, which I believe is a coincidence.

Name:	It's a Lottery
Code:	WT9806
Origin:	12 November 2001, New Jersey (USA)
Status:	True

UNCOVERED

The Legend

On 12 November 2001, the talk of New Jersey was the bizarre coincidence of their two 'Pick 3' lottery draws of that day. The morning numbers that were drawn were 5-7-8, and the draw later that day produced the numbers 5-8-7. These numbers make up the flight number of the American Airlines flight that crashed into the Queens area shortly after take-off on the same day that the numbers were drawn.

The Investigation

This amazing coincidence actually happened: the American Airlines flight number was 587. The news that there were lots of winners that day will not come as a shock to the hardened lottery player, as many people pick numbers that are associated with current events, signs or news stories. In fact, so many people picked the correct numbers on that day that the prize draw payout was only $16 per person, a lot lower than the average payout amount, which is about $275.

Eerily, although the New Jersey Lottery only usually held one draw per day, the day of the crash was the first time that two draws were held on the same day.

In another bizarre twist of fate, and one of the reasons for this UL's inclusion in the 9/11 section, the lottery numbers drawn in a New York state lottery on September 11th 2002, exactly a year after the terrorist attacks, were 9-1-1. Enough said.

And Finally...

A coincidence is a chance occurrence or set of events remarkable either for being simultaneous or for apparently being connected. But some people believe that there is no such thing as a chance occurrence and that everything happens for a reason. Without going into too much detail, the very building blocks of the universe and everything in it are made up of units of energy that produce electromagnetic forces. If every single thought that you have produces energy, and for every action there is a reaction, then maybe there is a real connection in the fact that someone starts humming out loud a tune that is in your head, or that you and your partner simultaneously say the same thing at the same time? Similarly, could there be some cosmic force at work that caused the lottery machine to eject the very same three numbers that made up the flight number of that ill-fated jet on the same day? Whether you agree with this theory or not, it does account for why people choose numbers for the lottery that have an association with a current affair, and in this instance it would appear that their theory paid off.

The plane crash on 12 November 2001 was not an act of terrorism and is not connected to the events of 9/11, but had a direct effect on the people of New York City, so soon after the terrorist attacks on the World Trade Center. The aircraft crashed in the New York area of Queens, a neighbourhood where many of the families of the firemen who lost their lives on September 11th lived. This crash must have opened emotional wounds that were barely starting to heal, and I can imagine this new tragedy would have been too much to bear for the friends and families involved.

Name:	Pentagon Attack
Code:	WT9807
Origin:	Thierry Meyssan, The Frightening Fraud
Status:	False

UNCOVERED

The Legend

On September 11th 2001, after the shocking news that the Twin Towers of the World Trade Center had been hit by aircraft, reports of an explosion at the Pentagon were filtering in. It was first reported that a large booby-trapped truck packed with explosives caused the blast, but later this was denied and the official account that an aircraft crashed into one side of the Pentagon was circulated.

It seems that there is more to this catastrophe than meets the eye, and more than a hint of a conspiracy theory. In fact, some question the existence of American Airlines Flight 77, and whether an aircraft did crash into the Pentagon at all.

So if an aircraft didn't crash into the Pentagon, what did? Why the cover-up, and who is behind it?

The Investigation

This ambitious conspiracy theory was first initiated by the French left-wing activist and author Thierry Meyssan, and published in his controversial book *The Frightening Fraud*.

Meyssan believes that the American government is covering something up, and that a plane did not cause the damage to the Pentagon. Many believe that he is blowing hot air, as he asks several probing questions but cannot supply any explanations as possible answers. Right or wrong, a conspiracy theory was born.

Hot on the trail, a website was created. The 'Hunt the Boeing!' website mirrored the claim of Thierry Meyssan that an aircraft did not crash into the Pentagon, and questions the official account of what actually happened. Like many conspiracies, the supporting 'evidence' is selective and therefore inconclusive. There now seem to be as many websites disputing the theory as those that are promoting it.

Some believe that the whole attack was orchestrated by the neoconservative movement. It is thought that the neoconservative membership boasts links to the most powerful and influential figures in US society, with one think tank pondering on the idea that the US government needs 'another Pearl Harbor' in order to carry out its objectives. Some neoconservatives believe that to effectively rule a country, you need the people to fear something. This theory was unwittingly put into practice during the Cold War, with the fight against Communism; cynics now believe that the US government exaggerated the danger and power of the Russians in order to plough ahead with its space program and controversial foreign policies. After the fall of the Berlin Wall and the collapse of Communism society needed a new enemy to fear, and another momentous event like Pearl Harbor had to happen for the people to realise that a new enemy was upon them. After 9/11, the US government was able to implement controversial strategies with full backing of its people under the guise of the war against terror. The cynics now believe that the neoconservatives have fulfilled their objectives.

And Finally...

I believe that denying the aircraft crashed into the Pentagon is an insult to the memory of those who lost their lives on Flight 77, especially for their friends and family. The conspiracy theory also fails to take into account the many eye witnesses who saw the crash happen.

Recently, official video footage was released of the moment of impact to debunk this conspiracy theory once and for all. Unfortunately, the footage does not clearly show an aircraft hitting the Pentagon. Without conclusive evidence, this conspiracy theory will continue to thrive.

Name:	The Birmingham Warning
Code:	WT9808
Origin:	Unknown
Status:	False

UNCOVERED

The Legend

This is not a joke or a hoax, this actually happened:

The other day I went around to my mate's house straight from work. His wife answered the door and her first words were not 'Hello' or 'Hi, how are you?' They were: 'Don't go into Birmingham on the sixth of October.' At first I thought she was joking, but I soon realised that she was deadly serious.

When we had all sat down, she started to explain how her friend was shopping in the cash and carry when a man of Arabic appearance standing in front of her in the check-out queue did not have enough cash to pay for his goods. Noticing that the man was only a few quid short, she offered to make up the difference. The Arab man seemed very grateful, and when they went out into the car park, he said to her, 'I would like to thank you for your kindness so I will give you this piece of advice; do not go into Birmingham centre on the sixth of October.'

Concerned by what she had just heard, the woman immediately contacted the police. They asked her to come down to the station and she was shown mug shots of local

287

known fundamental Islamic terrorism supporters. It was not long before she spotted the man that she had spoken to.

As I have already said, this is a true story and the police are taking it as a serious threat. It all may amount to nothing, but it is better to be safe than sorry.

The Investigation

This particular warning was rife at the end of September 2001, and was spreading via e-mail and word of mouth. The story was immediately condemned as a hoax, and the West Midlands Chief Constable, Edward Crew, stated that there is no intelligence to suggest there is any specific threat to the West Midlands. What is strange is that there was a terrorist bomb explosion in Birmingham city centre on 4 November 2001, but the attack was not carried out by an Islamic fundamentalist terrorist group, but by the Real IRA instead. Although eerie, this must have been a coincidence as there are many variations to the legend, and the origins of the 'warning from a stranger' legends go back years.

Another similar version was circulating in London at the same time as The Birmingham Warning. E-mails were rapidly being sent round offices telling a similar story, this time the shop in question was Harrods (a little bit more upmarket!), and the warning was not to travel on the Tube. This really was playing on people's fears, as a gas attack on the Tube is seen as a real and daunting potential threat.

In another variation a stranger warns of not going to Milton Keynes. In a city where everything has been created in block form, where the roads have more roundabouts than you could possibly imagine, and where the cows are even made out of concrete, I cannot imagine why anyone would want to go there anyway. Perhaps the hoax warnings are a conspiracy from disgruntled Wimbledon FC supporters against their team's move to Milton Keynes!

Coventry is another city that was targeted by this latest bout of e-mails, but there are many other places across the UK that have been used. In true UL fashion, the variations are often localised to make a bigger impact and so are designed to cause maximum panic. There is no rational reason to believe the stories as there is no evidence to back them up, but because of the real threat of fundamentalist Islamic terrorism sweeping the world, the stories are seized upon and spread rapidly.

Before 9/11, the same legends were told about warnings of IRA bombings on the mainland. In these legends the man giving the warning often spoke with a soft Irish accent.

'Warning from a stranger' legends go a lot further back than that, though, and the latest offerings may have evolved from legends like the one that was circulating around the USA just after the bombing of Pearl Harbor in World War Two. The story tells of a man giving a woman a lift in his car, and then refusing money that the lady has offered him for the petrol he has used. For this act of kindness, the woman offers to tell his fortune. She then predicts; 'There will be a dead body in your car before you get home, and Hitler will be dead in six months.' The man then supposedly came across a car crash on his way home and attempted to take a seriously injured man to the local hospital, but the man died of his injuries en route.

By the way, the other prediction about Hitler being dead in six months failed to come true.

And Finally...

Check out The Liverpool Warning, an amusing parody of this legend that arrived in my e-mail inbox late 2002, and is investigated on the Project 2067 website under the code PD7302.

Name:	The Coke Warning
Code:	WT9809
Origin:	2002
Status:	False

UNCOVERED

The Legend

A friend of my mother's was doing her weekly shopping at the local supermarket when a man who appeared to be of Arabic origin in front of her didn't have enough money to pay for his shopping. Noticing that the difference in amount was only about 50p, my mother's friend offered to settle the difference, which the man gratefully accepted.

When she was loading her shopping into the boot of her car, the Arab approached her and thanked her for helping him out and spoke these words of advice, 'Please, I must warn you, do not drink any Coca-Cola after the first of June.' With this he quickly left.

The Investigation

Sound familiar? This is basically another variation of the 'warning from a stranger' legends, very similar to the 'The Birmingham Warning' (WT9808). The difference being that in this particular one the warning is about a product and not a place.

The product in question is Coca-Cola, which makes this legend an interesting fusion between the typical 'warning from a stranger' legends and the old favourite Cokelore legends. The company's status as one of the most recognised products in the world has made it an easy target. Coca-Cola could be seen as a symbolic product of the Western world, and therefore a very believable target for fundamentalist Islamic terrorists hell-bent on causing a spectacular catastrophe that would match the events of 9/11. Cokelore is discussed in greater detail in the Food and Drink category. Check out the ULs Cokecaine (FD3306) and Santa Coke (FD3307).

And Finally...

The Coca-Cola website (Coca-Cola.com, not Coca-Cola.co.uk) states: 'These rumours are absolutely false and are causing needless worry.' The American-based website also debunks many other false rumours of Cokelore and is truly worth a visit.

Name:	Jackie Chan's Lucky Escape
Code:	WT9810
Origin:	September 2001
Status:	Undecided

UNCOVERED

The Legend

All actors typically curse late scripts, but this particular one proved a blessing in disguise. Martial arts star Jackie Chan was supposed to act out a scene for the filming of an action comedy movie called *Nosebleed*. The screenwriters delivered the script late, and Jackie, being the perfectionist that he is, decided to cancel that day's filming. Just as well, really, as the scene was scheduled to be filmed at 7 a.m. on the morning of September 11th 2001 on top of one of the World Trade Center's Twin Towers!

A shocked Jackie Chan quoted, 'I would probably have died if the shooting had gone ahead as planned.' Then adding in his trademark wry manner, 'Well, I guess my time is not up yet!'

Because of the delayed script for the film *Nosebleed*, Jackie altered his plans at the eleventh hour and started filming in Toronto for *The Tuxedo*.

The Investigation

News that Jackie Chan was to star in an upcoming film called *Nosebleed* was filtering through movie buff channels back in

1999. Earlier articles reported that the plot of the film was that Jackie Chan was to star as a window cleaner at the World Trade Center and accidentally overhears a terrorist plot to blow up the Statue of Liberty. Later, the plot was reported as Jackie Chan playing a window cleaner at the World Trade Center who takes a fancy to a waitress who works at the Windows of the World restaurant, which is situated at the top of the centre. Subsequently, the two get mixed up in a plot to blow up the World Trade Center.

Whichever one of the versions you choose to believe, the plot of *Nosebleed* is certainly eerie, but whether the shooting of the scene on top of the World Trade Center was scheduled and then cancelled for the morning of September 11th is debatable.

The story of Jackie's lucky escape was first picked up by Asian news sources and was reported in newspapers such as Singapore's *The Straits Times*, and was taken seriously enough to be documented in certain New York news sources as well. But one flaw in the legend has to be that *The Tuxedo* is reported to have been scheduled to start filming on 10 September 2001, one day before the supposed scheduled filming of *Nosebleed* on top of the World Trade Center. It is highly unlikely that the filming of a scene in New York for *Nosebleed* was scheduled for the morning after filming was due to start in Toronto on *The Tuxedo*. The film industry simply doesn't work in that way.

And Finally...

Lucky escape and strange coincidence stories can be heard on most movie sets, and movie ULs deserve to have their own category. This category would include legends such as those surrounding the suspicious death of Brandon Lee while filming

The Crow, and the mysterious ghost-like figure behind the net curtains in *Three Men and a Baby* (it turns out to be a cardboard cut-out of Ted Danson that was accidentally left on the set during the shooting of that scene).

Name:	The Devil's Face in the Smoke
Code:	WT9811
Origin:	September 11th 2001
Status:	Undecided

UNCOVERED

The Legend

Professional photographer Mark D. Phillips took photos of the World Trade Center from the top of his Brooklyn home less than three miles away just after the second aircraft hit. One of the photos appears to show a demonic face shaped out of the rising smoke from one of the towers.

The Investigation

Folk used to claim that a camera never lies, but in the age of digital technology we know differently. Images can be doctored, distorted, manipulated and airbrushed with such ease it can basically be achieved by any ten year old with a computer. Different images of the devil's face in the smoke have emerged since the terrorist attacks of 9/11, but most are thought to be fake. But the photograph taken by Mark D. Phillips is supposed to be 100 per cent genuine.

Mr Phillips has been a professional photographer for thirty years, having been a staff photographer for three newspapers and the Associated Press. The photo was one of many that were sold to the Associated Press and were transmitted within 40 minutes after the event. Mr Phillips informed me that he was attacked by his peers who questioned the authenticity of the digital image. Being digital, there is no film and so no negative, just a computerised original. However, the image has been verified by the digital camera manufacturer Olympus, whose brand was used to take the photograph.

OK. We now know that the photo is genuine, but what are we actually looking at? As always, it can be interpreted in many different ways. One theory is that it proves that Satan's power was resident in the World Trade Center. The image is 'proof' that Satan had been awakened and was fleeing his place of residence. The theory then claims that the World Trade Center was the root of all evil causing Third World debt, and the terrorists are actually martyrs ridding the world of evil.

The most popular belief is that the image of Satan appeared out of billowing smoke as a sign of the great act of evil that had taken place and as a warning of the evil that is at large in our world.

Of course, some may say that it is simply a coincidence, similar to seeing faces in the clouds. Whatever you believe, the photo taken by Mr Phillips has certainly generated a few lively debates.

And Finally...

Draw your own conclusions: visit the Mark D. Phillips website at www.markdphillips.com, or you can view the picture of the devil's face in the smoke by using the UL code on the Project 2067 website: www.project2067.com.

CATEGORY: PARODIES

In UL terms a parody is an imitation legend used for comical effect. A parody legend may contain segments from all different kinds of ULs, cleverly moulded together into an amusing tale. For a good example I must warn you about a new computer virus that may find its way into your inbox called the 'Gullibility Virus'. As soon as it is opened it makes people believe and forward copies of ridiculous hoax e-mails detailing anything from cookie recipes, Internet taxes and computer viruses to Nostradamus predictions and warnings from strangers in exchange for a kind deed. Once infected, the immune system to hoaxes and tall stories completely breaks down, and you end up believing anything you read on the Internet. This is not a hoax, and you can tell how serious this is by the number of exclamation marks I am using!!!!!!!! Please pass this message on to everyone you know. For every message forwarded, the Hopelessly Gullible Charity will donate one pound to itself!

As you may have guessed, the above warning is told with one eyebrow mischievously raised, but it does hit a chord of truth with the suggestion that people will believe anything they read on the Internet. This is an example of how parody legends use sarcasm and satire to entertaining effect. In other words, they take the Mick.

This is the last category that we will be exploring, and I have chosen Parodies to finish off on a light-hearted note: I hope you will find the following small collection amusing. Bin Laden's Memo (PD7301) is hilarious and comes as light relief from the hundreds of legends that have emerged from the events of 9/11. The Liverpool Warning (PD7302) follows in a similar vein, but is written with a serious tone and has a slight twist. Also worth mentioning is The UL Of ULs (PD7304). This is unique, as it is an accusation of a government conspiracy aimed at the UL websites that investigate and debunk legends. Confused? You will be!

Name:	Bin Laden's Memo
Code:	PD7301
Origin:	12 October 2001
Status:	False

UNCOVERED

The Legend

From: Bin Laden, Osama [mailto:osama@taliban.com]

Sent: Saturday, November 17, 2001 11.10AM

To: Cave mates

Subject: The Cave

Hi guys. I know that we've all been working really hard but I feel it's brought us closer as a group, and I love that. First up, a big thanks to Abdul for pinning up the poster that says, 'There is no "I" in team' and the one that says, 'Hang In There, Baby'. That monkey is so cute! But although we are fighting a Jihad, we still need to find time to look after the cave, and lately there's been some cause for concern.

For one thing, I know our main priority is cruise missiles, but I think the scorpions in our cave should be way up there too. Come on, no one wants to be stung, so we've got to start sweeping the cave every day. I've stuck a rota up near the cave entrance, and would appreciate it if you guys would sign and date it when this task has been done.

Secondly, on the rare occasion when I'm filming a video address, do bear in mind that I am trying to intimidate the most powerful country on earth. Therefore I'd appreciate it if you didn't ride around on your scooters in the background when we are doing a shoot. Thanks.

Third. A bit of a sensitive subject, this one. As I'm sure you are all aware, we are forbidden from shaving our beards. But come on guys, that's no excuse for skipping on hygiene, especially at mealtimes!

My fourth point, and this is a personal one: I bought a box of Wotsits recently, clearly labelled it 'Osama' and placed it on my food shelf. This Jihad can make me peckish and when I went to get a pack this morning, I found that they had gone. A bit of consideration. Enough said.

And finally, there have been reports of CIA spies in disguise trying to sneak into our group, so I'll be setting up patrols to flush them out. First on duty are Omar, Muhammad, Abdul, Akbar and Bob.

Love and hugs,
Osama

The Investigation

First aired on an American National Public Radio show called *Rewind* on the 12 October 2001, it soon spread globally in the form of e-mails. John Moe was the original author of this memo, and wrote it for *Rewind*, which is a satirical news program. It has been repeated on many other radio shows since, including the old *Chris Tarrant Morning Show* for Capital FM (London).

With the depressing shadow of global terrorism cast boldly over our heads, it is refreshing to see a satirical sideswipe at the whole situation. The thought of the most wanted man in the world running his camp of ruthless terrorists like a girl guide group brings a smile to my face.

Bin Laden's Memo is a parody of all the ULs, hoaxes and rumours associated with 9/11 and the hysteria that surrounds them. By turning the world's most wanted man into some sort of comical caricature, it helps to bring perspective to the situation and to calm our fears.

And Finally...

During World War Two, cartoons and songs about Adolf Hitler were used as propaganda by the allies. Hitler was portrayed as a silly little man with a ridiculous moustache, and one famous song even declared that 'Hitler has only got one ball, the other is in the Albert Hall'. It was this kind of humour that lifted the morale of the British people during the Blitz and helped keep alive the famous British spirit.

Name:	The Liverpool Warning
Code:	PD7302
Origin:	Unknown
Status:	False

UNCOVERED

The Legend

Normally I don't fall for this kind of thing, but a few people here have mentioned it and I think there could be something in it...

Beware!

I got this today and the warning is genuine!

Yesterday, a friend was travelling on a Paris to London flight. A man of Arabic appearance got off the plane and my friend noticed that he had left his bag behind. She grabbed the bag and ran after him, caught up with him in the terminal and handed him back his bag. He was extremely grateful and reached into his bag, which appeared to contain large bundles of money.

He glanced around to make sure nobody was looking and whispered, 'I can never repay your kindness, but I will try to... with a word of advice for you: stay away from Liverpool.'

My friend was genuinely terrified. 'Is there going to be an attack?' she asked him.

'No,' he whispered back, 'it's a sh*thole.'

The Investigation

This is a copy of an e-mail sent to me on 14 November 2002, and is a parody of The Birmingham Warning (WT9808). I thought this version was a typical 'warning from a stranger' UL until the very end, when the punchline caught me hook, line and sinker.

The Liverpool Warning came onto the scene just before the Christmas period, on the back of government warnings about possible terrorist attacks and advice to be vigilant at all times. It was a time of great anxiety and the UL emerged from a growing fear that the enemy is within.

This was a light-hearted poke in the eye of all the hoaxes and legends that were cluttering up our intrays, and provides humour in a very serious and sensitive climate. It is a subtle dig at how vulnerable and gullible we all are.

And Finally...

Liverpool isn't that bad... Honest!

Name:	Body Parts
Code:	PD7303
Origin:	Unknown
Status:	False

UNCOVERED

The Legend

Most of you have read the scare-mail about the person whose kidneys were stolen while he was passed out. While that was an urban legend, this one is NOT. It's happening every day. I'm sending this warning only to a few of my closest friends. You too may have been a victim... read on.

My thighs were stolen from me during the night of 3 August a few years ago. It was just that quick. I went to sleep in my body and woke up with someone else's thighs. The new ones had the texture of cooked oatmeal. Who would have done such a cruel thing to legs that had been wholly, if imperfectly, mine for years? Whose thighs were these? What happened to mine?

I spent the entire summer looking for them. I searched, in vain, at pools and beaches, anywhere I might find female limbs exposed. I became obsessed. I had nightmares filled with cellulite and flesh that turns to bumps in the night. Finally, hurt and angry, I resigned myself to living out my life in jeans and Marks and Spencer body shapers.

Then, just when my guard was down, the thieves struck again. My rear end was next. I knew it was the same gang, because they took pains to match my new rear end (although badly attached at least three inches lower than the original) to the thighs they had stuck me with earlier. Now my rear complemented my legs, lump for lump. Frantic, I prayed that long skirts would stay in fashion.

Two years ago I realised my arms had been switched. One morning while fixing my hair, I watched, horrified but fascinated, as the flesh of my upper arms swung to and fro with the motion of the hairbrush. This was really getting scary. My body was being replaced, cleverly and fiendishly, one section at a time. In the end, in deepening despair, I gave up my T-shirts.

What could they do to me next? I was being attacked, repeatedly and without warning. That's why I've decided to share my story. I can't take on the medical profession by myself. Women of the world, wake up and smell the coffee! That isn't really 'plastic' those surgeons are using. You know where they're getting those replacement parts, don't you? The next time you suspect someone has had a face 'lifted', look again! Was it lifted from you? Check out those tummy tucks and buttocks raisings. Look familiar? Are those your eyelids on that movie star? I think I finally may have found my thighs... and I hope that Cindy Crawford paid a really good price for them.

This is NOT a hoax! This is happening to women in every town every night.

...Warn your friends!!!!!!!

The Investigation

This story is a parody of The Kidney Heist (CR1708) and was obviously written by a woman who doesn't believe in growing old gracefully.

A close friend forwarded this e-mail to me on 21 November 2001, and he has no recollection of who sent him the original e-mail. The e-mail was written in very large font and was illustrated with cartoon-style characters – perhaps you have seen it yourself?

And Finally...

Not only had someone spent a lot of time putting this parody UL together, but the clever use of motifs from The Kidney Heist proves that they have an understanding of ULs and how they are used in the netlore medium.

Name:	The UL of ULs
Code:	PD7304
Origin:	Unknown
Status:	Undecided

UNCOVERED

The Legend

Research has proved that urban legend books and websites are actually urban legends themselves. It is said that these sources conversely declare stories are legends when they are actually true.

Why would anyone bother with such a deception? The reason is they are part of a global conspiracy to misinform the public. After all, what better way is there to cover up politically sensitive situations than to spread them as rumours and have them debunked as urban legends. This propaganda is directly targeted at the well educated and and is designed to deliberately manipulate the political 'think tanks' to deceive the public.

The registration address of many of the popular urban legend websites clearly shows a US government address. This address, usually the CIA, proves the US government's involvement in these sites. The CIA have made no official comment on these allegations, but off the record, one agent who wishes to remain anonymous stated, 'It is to keep the public informed on what they think they need to know, by debunking rumours and allegations as conspiracy theories or urban legends that could otherwise destabilise our present political environment'

Do not believe everything you read.

The Investigation

A conspiracy theory about the very people that supply us with information about conspiracy theories – whatever next? This theory originated from a document called The Dredged Report and is dated 2 January 1999, and can be found at the AFU and Urban Legends website (www.urbanlegends.com). It seems to me that this report is actually a spoof of The Drudge Report, which features cutting edge news by the infamous columnist Matt Drudge whose website is viewed by millions on a daily basis.

I love the ironic tone of this parody as it has turned the tables on the most popular UL websites on the Internet. It also brings up an interesting theory and triggers many 'What if?' questions. What if certain government agencies did control these websites? It is certainly possible, and this tactic could be used to debunk rumours that may be true but damaging to a country's interests. This would be an ingenious way to control the information that we are fed as it targets the very people that are sceptical of how much truth we are given and who thrive on conspiracy theories.

And Finally...

Who can you believe? As Mulder and Scully once said, 'The truth is out there!'

CONCLUSION

There is more to ULs than idle gossip told during those ritual 'office water cooler conversations' that take place at three o'clock in the afternoon in most offices, and those who know this can use them to their advantage. Used in the right way, a UL can be a very powerful psychological weapon, and the most obvious proof of this is when ULs are used as wartime propaganda. Hitler and Churchill both used the influence of ULs as a propaganda tool to full effect during World War Two, as they tried to outwit each other. Manipulation of this kind is a tried and tested technique but it is increasingly being used as a tactic in modern warfare. The American term for this tactic is 'psychops', a technique which was well documented during the Iraqi conflict of 2003. Indeed, what better way is there to boost morale at home or spread confusion and instigate unrest amongst enemy ranks than the spread of a well-designed but wholly concocted rumour?

There are other areas where the use of ULs can be exploited: the huge success of *The Blair Witch Project* just goes to prove that you do not need to spend millions of pounds on advertising campaigns to get a product noticed. But the power of ULs can also have the opposite effect for a company, with devastating consequences. In most situations it is unclear where these vicious rumours start from; they may be concocted by business rivals, or simply by someone with a grudge against that particular company. Large corporations such as Coca-Cola, KFC, Disney and Microsoft seem to be relentlessly targeted in what can only be described as hate campaigns. Some may see this as a justified stand against these huge, faceless corporations that have muscled smaller competitors out of their way to try and monopolise their particular markets; a typical David vs. Goliath scenario. People believe that certain corporations are not acting in the best interests of their customers because they are too consumed in their own greed and lust for money. Of course, it is still a dangerous game to play for any competitor, as it would be a huge PR disaster (not to mention libellous!) to get caught in the act.

Often, the origins of ULs are not so calculated and manufactured, but a reflection of the fears, anxieties and moral stand of a particular period in time. These ULs will appear again and again, decade after decade, adapting themselves to fit in with modern society, as is the case with many of the ULs I have included in the Classic Horror section.

The arrival of netlore has permanently changed the face of ULs. Some academics believe that the Internet has killed off the UL as we knew it, as it is now more about popular culture and less about folklore. It is true that hearing a story from a friend is far more interesting than reading it on a monitor screen, as the computer lacks the interactive effect of facial expressions and gestures that help bring colour to a tale, not to mention the social aspect. On the other hand, the Internet has helped to accelerate the spread of ULs on the global scene at lightning speed, although it's true that forwarded e-mails probably mean that there is a decrease in variation of each

UL because the text remains the same in each e-mail and the 'Chinese Whispers' effect is not applied. For anyone with an interest in ULs, the Internet has made research so much more accessible with superb websites including Snopes.com, although websites can never be a substitute for books such as the ones written by Jan Harold Brunvand.

Just as a UL may change and adapt to present situations, the whole structure and medium of ULs must do the same. Maybe the resentment of netlore is another manifestation of people's fear of new technology. I do not feel that the growth of netlore is a threat to the traditional UL; it is a mere change in direction to keep up with the ever-shifting sands of time.

As with most subjects under the sun, ULs can be dissected with a scientific approach. One scientific definition for ULs is that they are 'mind viruses'. This is a good definition as there are strong similarities. Just like a virus, ULs usually appear inexplicably and spontaneously spread from person to person, with the number of people it 'infects' multiplying after each case. The closer in proximity the versions are to the original UL, the less likely they are to vary from each other. The versions will vary to a greater extent as they move further away from their origin.

In the course of this investigation, we have only scratched the surface of ULs, but it has been enough to understand their mechanism and structure, how they are spread, and how they are effectively used for moral and propaganda purposes. You should also now be able to spot the traits of a UL when you read or are being told a story, and this will help in the prevention of spreading harmful rumours or bogus virus alerts. Just remember, if it happened to a friend of a friend, the story is probably as viable as Elvis driving a No. 57 bus through Tooting High Street, and if the story is too good to be true, then it probably isn't!

I hope you have enjoyed this investigation as much as I have – I think it has been a learning curve for all of us. But this is far from the end; it is just the beginning. To continue the investigation visit www.project2067.com.

BUZZWORDS AND JARGON

Sometimes it may seem that people in the UL circle are speaking in code, and you feel like you are trying to infiltrate some kind of secret society. Like in any interest, hobby, sport or subject, the small world of ULs does have its own terminology. The following is a short list of Urban Legend jargon and buzzwords and their meanings:

Terms used for 'urban legend':

Contemporary folklore
Dead Cat story
FOAF
Kentucky Fried Rat story
Modern folklore
Monkey Burger
Office water cooler conversation
UL
Urban myth
Urban folklore

FOAF: Friend of a Friend. Term coined meaning UL, as usually they begin with 'This happened to a friend of a friend...'

Monkey Burgers: ULs in the Netherlands are called 'broodje aap verhalen', which translates into English as 'monkey burgers'.

Proto-legend: A potential legend at the early stage of the process, that may or may not turn into a UL.

Netlore: ULs that are narrated with the use of e-mail and the Internet.

Faxlore: Term used when a UL is narrated with the use of a fax machine. Once a popular medium for ULs, it has now been completely overshadowed by netlore.

Motif: Common subject matter found in all versions of a UL and across different legends. For example, The Hook has the motif of a maniac with a hook for a hand.

USEFUL RESOURCES

Researching the origins of ULs is a long and painstaking business, if not sometimes impossible, but there are certain books and websites out there that may make life a little easier. The people who have written these books and websites are often experts in the field and have dedicated their lives to the research of ULs. You probably noticed that I have mentioned Jan Harold Brunvand a few times throughout the project and I have listed a few of his books below. In truth, any one of his many books would be a worthy read as they are not only interesting, but also written in a concise and clear manner. Jan H. Brunvand was a professor at the University of Utah and is extremely well respected in UL circles, but unfortunately he will not be writing any more books as he is now retired. I wish him the very best in his retirement and would like to thank him for his help when it was requested.

Books:

Title: *The Vanishing Hitch-hiker*
Author: Jan Harold Brunvand
Published by: W. W. Norton & Company

Jan H. Brunvand's first book and a must for anyone with even the slightest interest in ULs. First published in 1981, this book gives a thorough and interesting insight into all the classics. The book also contains an excellent chapter named 'Collecting and Studying Urban Legends'.

Title: *The Baby Train*
Author: Jan Harold Brunvand
Published by: W. W. Norton & Company

The Baby Train is a no-nonsense collection of ULs and their meanings. Worth buying for the 'A Type-Index of Urban Legends' section.

Title: *Too Good To Be True*
Author: Jan Harold Brunvand
Published by: W. W. Norton & Company

A large and colourful collection of ULs and their meanings, in a well-thought-out format.

Title: *Urban Legends*
Author: N. E. Genge
Published by: Three Rivers Press, New York

The book is an interesting read, although individual legends cannot be easily located, and the style of writing can sometimes be disjointed and confusing.

Title: *Alligators in the Sewer and 222 Other Urban Legends*
Author: Thomas J. Craughwell
Published by: Black Dog & Leventhal Publishers

This easy-read book is written in a stylish and well-organised manner. Its only let-down is the fact that no meanings or origins of the legends are offered.

Websites:

Website name: Snopes
Website address: www.snopes.com

This well-designed website is comprehensive and easy to navigate, but most importantly, it is simply the best source for information concerning ULs that you will find on the net.

Website name: The AFU and Urban Legends Archive
Website address: http://tafkac.org/

A large and comprehensive archive of ULs with a couple of cool features. The best probably being the Urban Legend Zeitgeist, where you can check out all the latest ULs. Another being the Urban Legend Vortex, where you can study ULs from the different hemispheres.

Website name: Urban Legends.about
Website address: www.urbanlegends.about.com

Easy to navigate but not in the same ball park as Snopes. Still worth a visit.

Website name: Broodje Aap
Website address: www.broodjeaap.nl

This is a newer version of the original Monkey Burgers website created by the colourful Patrick Arink as mentioned in Cleaning Up With Toothpaste (AW1909). This Dutch website is a big improvement on the original, but you will have to speak the lingo!

Website name: Official Darwin Awards/legends
Website address: www.darwinawards.com

Part of the official Darwin Awards website, this section deals with apocryphal stories of bogus Darwinian efforts.

Website name: Warphead
Website address: www.warphead.com

Cool website. Worth a visit but has a slightly confusing layout.

Website name: Urban Legends Online
Website address: www.urbanlegendsonline.com

Nice local legends section with the legends based in New Jersey (US).

[REVISED AND UPDATED]

CONSPIRACY THEORIES
Kate Tuckett
£5.99

ISBN: 1-84024-394-5
ISBN 13: 978-1-84024-394-9

Just because you're paranoid doesn't mean they're not after you...

Worried that the world is run by a sinister cabal operating at the very highest level of government? You could just be right. Bringing together startling evidence on topics ranging from JFK to Bush, Roswell to Harry Potter, Chernobyl to the curse of the Kursk submarine and Bruce Lee's death to Space Shuttle Columbia, *Conspiracy Theories* has a cover-up for every occasion.

www.summersdale.com